S0-ARK-781

Journey *from* HEARTACHE *to* HOPE

True Stories of God's Miraculous Healing Power

Elizabeth G. Danielsen
Psalm 34:18

ELIZABETH G. DANIELSEN

WESTBOW®
PRESS
A DIVISION OF THOMAS NELSON
& ZONDERVAN

Copyright © 2015 Elizabeth G. Danielsen.

All rights reserved. No part of this book may be used or reproduced by any means, graphic, electronic, or mechanical, including photocopying, recording, taping or by any information storage retrieval system without the written permission of the publisher except in the case of brief quotations embodied in critical articles and reviews.

WestBow Press books may be ordered through booksellers or by contacting:

WestBow Press
A Division of Thomas Nelson & Zondervan
1663 Liberty Drive
Bloomington, IN 47403
www.westbowpress.com
1 (866) 928-1240

Because of the dynamic nature of the Internet, any web addresses or links contained in this book may have changed since publication and may no longer be valid. The views expressed in this work are solely those of the author and do not necessarily reflect the views of the publisher, and the publisher hereby disclaims any responsibility for them.

Scripture taken from the Holy Bible, NEW INTERNATIONAL VERSION®. Copyright © 1973, 1978, 1984 by Biblica, Inc. All rights reserved worldwide. Used by permission. NEW INTERNATIONAL VERSION® and NIV® are registered trademarks of Biblica, Inc. Use of either trademark for the offering of goods or services requires the prior written consent of Biblica US, Inc.

Any people depicted in stock imagery provided by Thinkstock are models, and such images are being used for illustrative purposes only. Certain stock imagery © Thinkstock.

ISBN: 978-1-4908-6107-4 (sc)
ISBN: 978-1-4908-6108-1 (e)

Library of Congress Control Number: 2014920917

Printed in the United States of America.

WestBow Press rev. date: 02/13/2015

Dedication

Journey from Heartache to Hope is dedicated to all those who have supported Spiritual Care Support Ministries with their prayers, time, and financial means. Every one of them has been an essential part of accomplishing the vision of providing hope and healing to those who have lost hope due to illness, grief, and personal losses, and to those who journey with them. It is also dedicated, as promised so many years ago, to Stephen Carroll, my first hospice patient.

Acknowledgements

I would like to thank the Lord for entrusting me with the vision of Spiritual Care Support Ministries. Without God's abiding presence, wisdom, and direction on a daily basis, it would have been impossible to accomplish what He has called us to do.

To my husband, Arvid, who has prayed for and supported me from the moment I shared the dream and vision with him, I am blessed to have you in my life. Thank you for joining me on this journey of faith.

I am grateful for Susan Amato, Susan Izzie, Danette Jennings, Cheryl Reynolds, and Dorothy Slaga who helped with the details to bring this book into being.

I especially want to thank all of our contributors for sharing their feelings, emotions, and experiences so that we can see the glory of God in their healing. When people are willing to open their hearts to others, we all can witness the grace and miracle of God's love. That's right! Miracles still do happen, and this book is a testament to the miracles of healing hearts. God is at work among us, and we are blessed.

Contents

Preface

In 1985 I spent days and nights by my terminally ill mother as she lay in her hospital bed. I quickly began to see the need for additional support for the sick and dying. In my vigil by my mother's bedside I heard patients crying in the night wanting someone to pray with them, to hold their hand and to listen to their emotional, physical, and spiritual pain. They needed someone to actively listen to and care about their life and eminent death. While sharing their personal stories with me in the night hours, it was so clear that they had so many unresolved issues that were never met. Many of the patients I spoke to never found healing.

After my mother died, our family moved from New Jersey to Houston, Texas, and it was then that I became a volunteer at the Houston Hospice. When we returned to New Jersey, I became a volunteer for the Karen Ann Quinlan Hospice. Eventually, I joined the staff and was their Hospice Volunteer Coordinator and became the KAQ Hospice Chaplain. I gained a vast amount of knowledge at the bedsides of hospice patients and continued my education to become a hospital chaplain, receiving my ministerial credentials for ordination and becoming a Nationally Endorsed Health Care Chaplain.

I have spent many hours with those suffering emotional, physical, and spiritual pain. I heard multiple times about the lack of support, emotional care, and understanding of the challenges patients were facing. Their spiritual and emotional needs were not being met. This caused many to turn away from their families, faith communities, and from God at a time when they should have been adamantly seeking His love and care.

In 1989 the Lord gave me a vision for Spiritual Care Support Ministries and a ministry center. The center would be a place to assist people who suffer from the emotional, physical, and spiritual pain of loss in their lives. These losses are derived from declining health, loss of a loved one, divorce, etc. The center would provide the support they need to heal emotionally. I went to bed praying because I had a burden. God blessed me with a dream and then the vision of SCSM. Those suffering pain would be given a faith perspective and guidance towards the healing power of God. This ministry would also equip qualified individuals to effectively counsel and teach those in need of healing and hope.

On March 5, 2004, Spiritual Care Support Ministries incorporated. On May 1, the doors to the Center opened at 76 West Shirley Avenue, Warrenton, Virginia. On September 17 and 18 of that year, the official ribbon cutting ceremony and open house were celebrated.

The fulfillment of a promise, the realization of a dream.

A Note From the Illustrator

Susan Izzie

To me, a tree represents the complexity and unpredictability of life. Without the roots, the tree would die. Without our faith in God, our soul would die. God provides the sustenance that travels through the tree and our lives. He knows which branches will grow, which will wither, and when new growth will occur. People never have control of the scenarios of their losses. We rely on God to lead us through the twists and turns of life. When we think the tree may die, God frequently starts new growth in unexpected places as we, His children, find healing in unexpected ways. We cannot flourish alone.

A tree is a beautiful creation of God and, like us, no two are the same. We are beautifully and intricately made.

Susan R. Izzie
Illustrator

Introduction

Emotional pain is one of the most misunderstood emotions in the human race. If you have not experienced it, it is a foreign concept. If you have experienced pain, it is inconceivable that you will ever find healing. Few people know how to respond to the pain of another or how to cope when we feel it ourselves. We frequently avoid those who are hurting because of our lack of knowledge. We feel abandoned when we find ourselves in the position of needing comfort because others don't know how to react to our emotions. Where can you find solace, spiritual guidance, and education? Where do we find God in all that we are experiencing?

It is important that people who are in need of healing find a place that has the necessary tools to assist them in moving past the pain. We are frequently asked for clarification as to the purpose of this ministry. We can explain what our mission, vision, and values statements are but more information and clarification is often required for true understanding to take place. Perhaps you who are reading this introduction need more information as well.

The greatest loss one can experience is the loss of a loved one, a pain that is not imaginable until we experience it in our own lives. This is a loss that can affect every aspect of our lives and can frequently lead to deep depression and anxiety as unresolved issues go with us from year to year. Where do we go? What do we do? Should we suffer alone to spare others from pain, or should we seek assistance for this life-changing event?

Spiritual Care Support Ministries is here to bring understanding, hope, spiritual guidance, and support to those suffering loss in their lives. We are here to support those who come to us until they make the decision to begin living again because they have found purpose.

We are not an addiction center, although we know of centers that specialize in treating those with addictions. However, we can help those who are journeying with those suffering from addiction. We are able to assist family members who have experienced losses due to the addictions that have affected their lives.

We are not a marriage counseling center. However, we do help couples who are having marriage difficulties due to past losses in their lives.

We work with children six years and older who have had losses, but we are not able to help children who have been diagnosed with emotional or learning disabilities, etc. We do, however, work with the family members affected by these disabilities that may cause the loss of positive hope for their child's future and negatively affect their family relationships.

We assist clients experiencing job loss, loss of health, loss of identity, infidelity, loss due to miscarriage and still births, loss of dreams, loss of friendships, financial loss, and the list goes on.

The stories contained here are true and written by the individuals affected. These stories portray pain that at times seems unbearable but nonetheless portray the experiences of the writers, individuals who have journeyed from heartache to hope.

God has called us to this very specific ministry where we provide support and education to those who are ill, dying, experiencing grief and personal losses, and those who are journeying with them. We are called to equip and train others so they can effectively bring emotional assistance and guidance to others. That is our calling, and I am so thankful to the eighty Spiritual Care Support Ministries volunteers who understand what we do and are a part of this ministry. If you have any questions about SCSM, please do not hesitate to contact me at ChaplainLiz@scsm.tv.

CHAPTER 1

Broken Branches of Loss

When the tree is battered and beaten by the storms of life, some limbs will be become damaged and lose the will to stay attached. They sometimes require extra assistance to maintain their hold on the one thing that keeps them alive and experiencing growth.

Loss can devastate and destroy us; heart, mind, and body if we allow it. We must be guided by knowledgeable people who understand the way out of this dark and bleak place and can guide us back to the light of Christ. He is the only true physician and awaits our cries of despair. He will slowly heal our hearts so that we may again find joy in His presence.

These are stories of loss, pain, and often the struggle to stay attached. Healing is frequently a long, twisted journey with many barriers to overcome. It requires patience and understanding to travel this road with them, but that is what God has called us to do. Love one another.

Joe Who?

Joe Toth

Walking, walking, and walking. I do a lot of walking now. Walking seems to make the world slow down. It is peaceful. It is a time for thinking. It is a time for remembering. It is also a time for praying and talking to God. This is what I do now since my wife of forty-eight years succumbed to cancer.

I was walking through my neighborhood not long ago when I noticed a personalized license plate with "JANEWHO" on it. While I do not know who owns the car, I thought, *That is me! JOE WHO!* Before the death of my wife, it was always Carolyn and Joe, Joe and Carolyn, Mr. and Mrs., or my wife and I. You know the drill. Perhaps that is how you think of yourself - part of the JANEWHO crowd. Perhaps you have been able to move on and have created a new identity for yourself and no longer belong to the fraternity of JANEWHO.

I know it is going to take time. Time to heal, time to get past this grief, time to move on, time to create a new identity, time to...

How do I know this? I know this because I know God will help me through it, and I have seen it happen before my eyes many, many times. I know this because I co-facilitated bereavement support groups for seven or eight years at Spiritual Care Support Ministries. I have seen what grief can do to people and the crippling effect it has on them.

I have also seen the awaking of those suffering from grief and moving on with their lives. So, when my wife was diagnosed with cancer six years ago and only given a ten percent chance of living two years, I started to absorb everything from those support groups, knowing that sometime soon it would be me. It would be me in the shoes of those who just lost a loved one and did not know if they could make it to tomorrow. Unlike them, I would be prepared. Oh, how wrong I was.

I was as wrong as the doctor who originally diagnosed her with stage four colon cancer and said she had little or no chance of making it another two years. I was as wrong as her primary care doctor who advised her not to get chemo but to let nature take its course. Of course, they did not know my wife, Carolyn. They did not know her faith and trust in God. They did not know her inner strength. They did not know her courage. They did not know her will to live. They did not know her love for me, our daughters, sons-in-laws, grandchildren, and the rest of our family and friends. Most of all, they did not know her love of being wherever she was at the time. They were amazed at her attitude and her constant smile. Whatever they threw at her, she took it without complaining and stood up wanting more. They could not believe she did not have pain. Unfortunately, neither did I. It was not until her final stay in the hospital that I learned otherwise.

I was told her lungs were failing and she only had hours—or best case, days—to live. When we first got married we promised each other that no matter how terrible things got, we would always tell each other the truth. So, I relayed to her what the doctor told me. She looked at me and asked, "Is that why it hurts so badly?" It virtually floored me when she said that. It was all I could do to keep from totally breaking down in front of her. To this day I wonder how long she hid the pain and where she got the strength to do so.

She was, without a doubt, the most remarkable person I have ever met. I thank God daily for the many wonderful days we had together since we met fifty years ago. I know I forget many things as I age, but I truly cannot remember a bad day we had together. Even the day I told her she had cancer was a good day. When I told her, she cried for two or three minutes and then looked me in the eye and said, "I am going to beat this." She never cried again, and she did beat it for six years. Unfortunately, the human body can only take so much. The cancer, along with the over 150 chemo treatments, finally took her from us. She will never be forgotten, and I cannot wait for the day I will meet up with her again. The next time we meet will be forever.

As I mentioned earlier, I had been preparing for Carolyn's death for over six years, and I thought I was ready. Boy was I wrong. The grief was overwhelming. I have slowly been able to handle it and am starting to get away from its grip. What I was not ready for was the loneliness and what to do with myself and the rest of my life. I was not ready for the guilt that was building up inside of me.

I was her caregiver for the last six years and spent nearly every minute with her. I was there for every chemo session, every doctor visit, every test, every high, and every low. Many people describe it as a roller coaster ride, and it truly was. As someone says in one of the videos we watch at the bereavement support groups, "I was prepared to continue to take care of her and not for her death."

Doubt keeps running through my mind asking if there was something more I could have or should have done. Was she in pain because I encouraged her to stay on this earth with us? Why did I not insist she have a colonoscopy much earlier? These are questions that will haunt me the rest of my life.

These questions are small in comparison to my biggest guilt of all, and that is the decision I made not to resuscitate her once her heart stopped. We had previously talked about dying. We had talked about almost all scenarios, and we both decided we did not want to continue living by artificial means. But for some reason we never talked about resuscitation. When the doctors first mentioned it to me, I said, "Yes, resuscitate her." I discussed it over and over again with the medical staff as to whether or not to resuscitate her. I finally decided it was not an option. I asked them to put her on morphine and not to resuscitate her once her heart stopped.

My biggest regret of all is not being there when they put a big green band on her wrist that read "DNR." The nurse stopped by to give her a bath, and I stepped out to get a coffee. When I returned she had this band with the giant DNR on her wrist. I can only imagine what went through her mind when they did that.

As usual, she was smiling when I returned and did not mention the band. So I do not know if she knew what the band meant, was simply saying she was okay with it, or asking why I was giving up on her. I want to think that she knew and was saying she was ready.

I know it honestly does not matter as I would do it the same way if I had to do it again, but I would instruct them not to put on the band until I was present. However, that does not ease the pain. I know it is something I will have to live with until the fantastic fifty years I knew and deeply loved her replaces the hurt and guilt. I know God will see that it does.

I also know that she was a woman of her word. If she said she would do something, you could count on it. When I told her that she was not getting out of the hospital, the first thing she asked me was if our daughters knew. I said they knew. She replied with a smile, "okay," and accepted it just like she did everything else. I asked if she would do one last thing for me. She asked me what it was. I told her that I wanted her to be waiting for me when I crossed over. She grabbed my hand and said, "I will be the first one you see," and I know she will keep her word.

Sweet Memories

Karen Angell

It is with many sweet memories that I write this. Ten years ago today, our Michael Arc Angell was killed, taken from us at the age of forty-three. Too young, too quick, too soon! Those of us who knew him best and loved him most were devastated. For those who did not know Mike, or did not know him well, he was someone you'd never forget. He lived life every day to the fullest. He never missed the opportunity to make a friend and provide better for his family. He was a true go-getter. He gave his all in everything he did, including church, family, work, and sports. Mike had no time for laziness or quitters. Not perfect, he often reflected on how to be a better Christian, husband, father, and friend.

A story not known to many, the night before he was killed we had a conversation about our life. We both spoke of how we had no regrets about our love for one another, the home and community we chose to live in, the five beautiful children that we shared, and the life we were living. I was blessed with that conversation. I know that when he left me, he loved his life, but I still questioned God. How could He take someone so young, with so much to give, and who loved being here?

I've learned through these ten years that many of our questions are not answered. You can ask all you want, but only time will glean some of the answers but certainly not all. I have also learned that I have little, if any, control over anything! Raising five teens surely drove that home! But through it all, I have loved this journey. The strength that I have needed has only been there because I signed up with God long ago. He has been with me from the beginning, and I have no qualms about leaning on Him. I also give great credit to my wonderful brothers and Mike's siblings. My friends and unknown community members have given time, money, kind gestures, and a warm hug. There are not enough words to ever thank you all for being there for us.

My children have been the reason I am able to move forward. I believe their journey is much more difficult than mine. To not be raised with a dad is a pain I can never understand. But like their dad, they have lived up to his legacy, following their own dreams and speaking their own minds. They are five beautiful, bright, lively, funny young people. I adore them! So, my message for whoever may read this is to take the time *right now* to call, visit, hug, speak to, play with, text, chat, IM, or twitter any and all the people in your life that you love! Remind them of how much you love, respect, and care for them. Do not leave yourself open for regrets. No way to live, no way to die. Enjoy the journey, work hard, play often, and love well!

What God Can Do With Daisies

JoAnn Ballengee

Several days before Mother's Day, I was feeling really low and missing my son, Troy, and my mom deeply. I was also struggling with a general disdain for the dreaded month of May. I think it is an especially difficult time for me, not only due to Mother's Day, but also because it is the same month sweet Troy went to heaven at the age of three and a half years. Yet I knew that God would bring a blessing out of this rough day as always, and reminded myself to be alert and ready to recognize it.

And the day before Mother's Day, it happened!

After work that day I went to Walmart to do my yearly shopping for flowers to plant in Troy's wagon. I wanted something different this year, and an orange Gerbera Daisy caught my eye. I thought it would make a nice center for the arrangement and placed several in my cart. As I turned to continue loading flats of other various flowers, I saw a nine or ten year old little girl touching one of the daisies in my cart.

"Excuse me," she said tentatively and then went silent due to nervousness. "She wants to know where you found that flower," her mother explained.

I pointed to the table and the little girl said, "Thank you!" as she ran in that direction. When she reached the table, she again called out, "Thank you!" I smiled, and as I finished my selections, I was struck by an overwhelming urgency to buy that flower for her. I knew with absolute certainty that this was what God wanted me to do. I never have cash on me, so I decided I would get some at checkout and go back and give it to her.

The checkout line was long, and I began to wonder if I would miss the opportunity to find the little girl. Then I remembered who was in charge of this mission and told myself it would work out! When I finally finished my purchase and got the cash, I immediately went back into the lawn & garden area but she was no longer there. Not to be defeated, I went to load up my car and returned to the store with the confidence that God would lead me to her. Then a bit of panic began to creep in as I looked down each aisle. *What if she hugs me? I don't know if I can do this without falling apart! Oh, Lord - help me! I don't even know if I can speak without bawling, but I want to obey you. Help me!*

Suddenly she was a few feet from me, her face lighting up with glad recognition as she waved and said, "Hi!" I told her I wanted to buy the flower for her and placed the money in her hand. She responded with an enthusiastic, "Thank you!" Her mother appreciatively said I didn't have to, but I said, "Oh, I *want* to!" The little girl then said, "Now, give me a hug!" We shared a big, sweet hug. I looked them both straight in the eye, smiled and said, "God bless you," and walked away.

As I left the store, I was laughing and crying at the same time. I was laughing because God can use a flower to bring healing to some and joy to others. I was crying because He used me to do it, and I realized how far He had brought me in my grief and faith journeys (thus far!). Little things can be the beginning of great works. Just by saying three little words with deepest sincerity to that little girl and her mother may be a start for them. I pray it is.

When I got to my car, I wept unabashedly and thanked God for the opportunity to touch someone's life in such a simple way. It was so freeing to obey Him and to have no need to tell my story. I will treasure that day's blessing the rest of my life, and I vow to always have cash in my pocket so I will never miss any that will come in the future!

May you smile and give God thanks every time you see a daisy.

Our Son, Ryan

Darlene Goodwin

Ryan was my life and my joy. For years it was just Ryan and me, having fun, doing homework, and going to church. I was Ryan's mom, and we were always there for each other. He loved me and always wanted to protect me. He was very musically talented, playing the guitar and singing. God had placed an anointing on his life, and I believed God was going to use him to do great things in the lives of others.

As Ryan grew older, he struggled with depression and eventually a heroin addiction. Oh, how I prayed for Ryan. I would not leave God alone. I was desperate for help, deliverance, and healing. Yet my ultimate prayer was for Ryan to spend eternity in heaven. I remember telling the Lord that it would be ok to take him as long as he was saved. Sometimes I wonder how I could have prayed that, but I was willing to give him up if it meant he would be in heaven for eternity.

Heroin had a stronghold on Ryan's life and it did not want to let go. We tried everything and spent a lot of money doing it. Rehabs, doctors, courts, and medicines didn't work but prayer did!

Ryan gave his heart to the Lord in March 2006. This time his life changed dramatically. Everyone noticed the difference in him. He told everyone how the Lord had changed his life and saved him, but things were not easy. He wrecked his car, work was slow, and life was lonely, but he stayed clean.

Early on Saturday morning I went to wake Ryan for a meeting. No answer. I tried his door but it was locked. A bad feeling washed over me. As I went into his room, I saw Ryan "asleep" on his couch with a needle lying in his lap.

The unthinkable had happened. On June 3, 2006, my precious son had died at the age of twenty-two. I believe the stress, sadness, and loneliness had closed in on Ryan. In looking for a bit of relief, he had used drugs.

How do I tell you how loyal God has been through all of this?

God has been so wonderful through all of this. He continues to give us a peace that we cannot understand or comprehend. It has truly been a difficult time, a true trial, but God does all things well! My prayer has been answered as I know I will see my son in heaven one day soon.

God has been so gracious to give my mom a vision of Ryan walking hand in hand with Jesus. I also had a dream of Ryan coming up to me, holding me, and then saying, "Mom, I never meant for all of this to happen." I said, "Ryan, are you in heaven?" He said, "Yes." Then he was gone. The last dream I had was on the one year anniversary of Ryan's death. I dreamed I followed Ryan into his room, which was flooded with light. We sat down and then I noticed his brand new shoes. These shoes were so different, so shiny, so clean and spotless!

Our lives were devastated when Ryan died. We had no idea how to deal with such a loss. We were in shock, not knowing what to do or where to turn. What we did know was that God was there for us through our families, friends, church, and through SCSM. While planning the funeral, our pastor told us about SCSM and gave us Liz Danielsen's phone number. Liz assured us they would be there to help us through the most difficult time in our lives.

In September 2006 we started attending the Grief Group meeting at SCSM. Through the love we received, God ministered to us, and we found acceptance, support and spiritual guidance. No one at SCSM looked down on us because our son died from a heroin overdose. This place has been a refuge for our souls, a stream in the desert.

How do I begin to explain the new hope that is now in our hearts or the dreams that have laid dormant for twenty years that are now coming to life?

Our dream is based on Isaiah 61:1-4 which talks about how God wants to use us to bind up the brokenhearted, comfort all who mourn, give beauty for ashes, the oil of joy for mourning, the garment of praise for the spirit of heaviness, and to restore the places which have been devastated.

We are so excited to be facilitating the Bereaved Parents Group on the first and third Saturday mornings of every month. We want to share in the lives of grieving parents who are hurting just like we were. Our struggle is not over, but it has become easier as we have joined hands with others who have walked the same difficult path. It is our prayer that God will use our lives to bind up your broken heart and that He will be glorified.

From a Teen's Heart

Charlene Hammarberg Stein

One December night in 2004, I got the terrifying news that my dad might have cancer. I was overwhelmed with all kinds of emotions, including anger and frustration. I thought to myself, "I just went through this with my best friend."

My best friend's dad died of cancer the previous year. I comforted and walked alongside her for three years as he battled with the cancer. I thought to myself, "God, it was hard enough then. Please, not MY dad!"

I called many people, crying and asking them just to pray. One evening the dreaded news I hoped would never come came. My dad had esophagus cancer. I went through periods of denial and frustration as I thought about my dad's cancer. I was assured by both my parents and the doctors that my dad was going to be okay and his chance of dying was low. People kept telling me that I was lucky because at least he didn't have a really aggressive kind of cancer. In January my dad had a feeding tube put in and underwent chemo and radiation.

Life went on and my dad was scheduled for surgery to remove three-fourths of his esophagus on April 26, 2005, at Johns Hopkins Hospital. To my surprise and disappointment, they were unable to do the surgery. The only thing that I heard was that my father's cancer had spread, and they would have to see the chemo doctor when they got home. About two weeks later they met with the doctor and he told us that my dad had about three to four months to live. They told us we had the option of putting him through

14

extensive experimental chemotherapy to see if that would help at all. We decided to take that route. A little over a week later, my dad went into the hospital with a bowel obstruction, and they told us the cancer had spread all over his body. They told us my dad only had about a day to live.

However, we were blessed and had four awesome days with my dad. On May 23, 2005, my father passed away. I was devastated. Many times I questioned, "Why God? Why would you do this to me?" I did not understand then and still do not fully understand. I just try to remember that God is in control. My father was not just my father, he was my best friend.

Beginning my senior year in high school has been very hard without my father, but God and various people are helping me get through it. Life is not easy. I am told things will get better as time goes by. I am not so sure. I miss my daddy more and more each day.

This past Christmas was the first Christmas without my dear father, Arnold Hammarberg. Christmas came seven months after my father passed away. Many people would come up to my family and say, "Your Christmas is going to be really hard." We didn't want to hear that.

With the anticipation of Christmas being very hard and just not the same without my father, I went into the Christmas season with a feeling of apprehension. I did not know what this Christmas was going to be like, but I figured it would be extremely hard.

To my surprise, my Christmas went much better than expected. I went into the Christmas holiday with a feeling of loneliness without my father, but also a reassurance that my dad was in heaven with a new healthy body and having a lot of fun. Like my older sister said, "If dad was still here, Christmas would have been much harder for us because he would have had such a poor quality of life." My mother said the hardest thing for her this Christmas was just putting "From Mom" on the gifts. After wrapping all the Christmas gifts, a friend told my mother she should have just put a heart representing love.

This Christmas my family ordered some really nice flowers. On my mother's birthday, December 23, my mother, brother, sister, and I delivered these very special flowers to my father's grave, placing them there in honor of his life. Next year my family is going to put up a Christmas tree there in memory of him.

Christmas was not the same, but we all know where my father is and there is no doubt about that. My daddy was my hero, and I am assured that one day I will see my hero again. One day I will be able to run to my daddy and sit on his lap again.

God allowed me to go through the situation with my best friend and her dad for a reason. God knew all along. This has been the most devastating time of my life, but I just keep trusting God.

I have encouraged many of my friends to spend as much time with their parents as they can. This time last year I didn't know I would not have my father anymore. Through all of this, I have learned that you do not know when death will come, but we all need to be ready.

Hearing His Name

Jeanette Meadows

On May 11, 2006, at thirty-two weeks gestation, my son Eric Curtis Meadows was delivered stillborn. I had learned during a routine twenty week prenatal sonogram that my unborn child, my son, was anencephalic and would not survive. Doctors advised that I terminate the pregnancy. Faced with that decision, I prayerfully chose to continue on, uncertain of how the events of the weeks ahead of me would unfold and if I would be able to survive the heartbreak and pain. I was hurt, disappointed, confused, and frightened. How could this have happened to me, to my baby? I am the mother of four healthy children. Why was this pregnancy unlike the others? What does one do when God doesn't make sense?

I am a preacher's kid, have been in church since I was born, and accepted the Lord Jesus Christ as my Savior at a very early age. I was filled with the Holy Spirit as a teen, but never was my walk with God more real than when I experienced the loss of my child. We had prayed for days following the diagnosis, praying for a miracle, praying that some error was made during the first sonogram. Even after a specialist had confirmed the diagnosis during a second sonogram, I would still find myself praying and hoping for a miracle. However, the miracle I was searching for was not the miracle God had planned for me.

Throughout the weeks, I was busy attempting to document as many memories of the pregnancy as I could, while also trying to prepare myself for the loss of my son and his impending burial.

On April 19, 2006, at about twenty-eight weeks pregnant, I was diagnosed with polyhydramnios. An excess amount of amniotic fluid was collecting in the amniotic sac. This was the result of the intrauterine growth restriction caused by the anencephaly. By this time I was becoming increasingly uncomfortable and had begun to worry about my own health.

I remember waking one morning and saying a prayer, "God, I am ready, take him home." The weekend came and went. Monday we were back at work. I will never forget that cold and rainy day in May. I recall sitting in a meeting and feeling uncomfortable. I remember placing my hand on my right rib cage, trying to apply pressure to ease the discomfort. What I didn't know at that time was that my baby had rested his head there. I went to the doctor for a visit on Wednesday of that week. In my heart I knew they would not find his heartbeat. I knew my baby had passed away.

We went into the hospital that afternoon to induce labor. They performed a sonogram before inducing my labor and it was as if my son was nestled in my arms, his head laying on my right side and his feet were to my left. I now was concerned that they would have to perform a c-section and I was frightened. They left the room to prepare an epidural while my father prayed.

I had the epidural and the doctors returned to attempt to manually turn the baby. They performed another sonogram before they began the process. To their surprise and ours, the baby was now in the correct position for labor and delivery. This was the miracle God had planned for me. How neat it was to hear my midwife say it was divine intervention. It was God! God just performed a miracle, in my hospital room, in my body.

On May 16th, 2006, we had a funeral service for our son. I spoke at the service and stated that, "I truly believe I understand God's purpose for this journey." I don't know if I completely did understand at that time or do now. I feel that God is still unveiling His purpose to me. I will always feel privileged that God chose me to carry an angel.

Through my support at Spiritual Care Support Ministries, I have been able to recognize my son's life. A child that survived in my womb for thirty-two weeks is now with God, perfect, and whole. I am thankful to SCSM for making a Christmas Tree Lighting Ceremony available. It was an honor to hear my son's name called among those that would have a light lit in their memory. Also, as a thank you for my donation made to SCSM in memory of my son, I received a bookmark that had my son's name printed across it. That bookmark is still in my Bible today. Any mom will tell you how wonderful it feels to see your child's name in print.

I am so thankful that I was greeted at SCSM by a caring and supportive staff who were there to help meet my needs as I went through what will be one of the hardest experiences in my life, the loss of a child.

The Journey

Vickie Richey

On November 18, 2004, my darling Gary died and that began the long, painful journey of grief and mourning. It's hard to explain what his loss has meant. The following is a segment from my journal on August 3, 2005:

> I can't be strong or perky or cheerful or brave. I don't care if I'm not a good example or if I'm a disappointment. I'm screaming with pain and loss.
>
> Heaven is foreign to me. It does not bring the comfort I expected. I only know it's far, far away and Gary is there—away from me. I can't see his face or hear his voice or touch his hand. He's gone. He's dead.
>
> It's sinking in. Past the layers of shock. My darling Gary is never, never coming back. Ever.
>
> These are words I despise—single, widow, change of status, alone, cemetery, a new start, moving, "how are you doing?"
>
> People are sick of me. I'm sick of me. I can't talk to anyone, not really talk. They'd be afraid of me.
>
> I'm exhausted from the trying—just trying to live, to work, to keep going.
>
> I'm surprised people can't see the huge, bleeding hole in the middle of my chest—the gaping place where Gary used to be. But he's gone and I can't get better. I can't recover. I've lost too much blood.
>
> My body continues to live, but I'm lost somewhere. So alone. I wish there was an escape hatch, but it's not there.

These are the emotions of grief. I'm glad they're not the truth.

In September 2005 I was invited to the SCSM Grief Group, which was the very best decision I could have made. It was the right time for me.

You are safe at Grief Group—no advice, no questions, and no judgment. There is loving support always, contact numbers for crisis times, a place to express, cry, laugh, share and reach out to other precious ones walking this long highway. You are also free to just be silent.

Grief Group is like having warm arms wrapped around you when you're shivering, like soothing ointment gently smoothed over a raw wound, or like a steady hand holding your quaking hand.

Grief Group is the shimmering, yet resilient thread of hope that is generously offered every week. It is a haven of comfort, healing, and safety. I *love* the wonderful people I have met there.

The God of Grief Group has ministered to me directly. He has never left me for a day of these most sorrowful and pain-filled of all my days.

Do I *feel* His presence? Not as much as I *experience* His presence. His presence and strength are experienced in being able to really live each day, including sleeping again, waking in the morning, and going to work.

I have learned simple things firsthand:

- Praise with a shattered heart and tears streaming down your face still belongs to God and it's still praise.
- God is patient. He has never hurried or pushed me.
- God is acquainted with grief. I don't have to explain it to Him. (Isaiah 53)
- The Lord is close to the brokenhearted. (Ps. 34:18)
- God is gentle. His voice is soft and whispery.
- God is comfort and shows compassion. (Ps. 119:76)
- God has faithfully *loved* me. (1 John 3:1)

God has cradled me in His arms. They're warm and strong and secure. He has assured me through His word that I *will* get better. Joy comes in the morning.

He has read my heart, not my lips. He has joined in my tears. He has never taken His eyes off me.

He is my anchor and my rock of refuge even when my emotions rock me.

I am grateful to this wonderful Father, the God of all peace.

My journey continues...

Unexpected Treasures

Dorothy Slaga

"Hey Mom! Guess what? I'm moving to Florida!"

"Huh? When?"

"In two weeks!"

My nest would be empty. It was August 1995 and my nineteen year old youngest child was leaving, having decided at the last minute to go to school in Florida. My heart ached.

We had just begun building our new home in Nokesville after a ten year wait on the Lord for the go-ahead. We were building next door to my parents to be able to help them now that they were in their mid eighties and slowing down. In September we put our house on the market. It sold that weekend—a lot sooner than we expected. We had to be out by Thanksgiving. The new house was supposed to be ready sometime in December, so we'd just move in with my parents for a short while.

Meanwhile, I quit the job I'd had for about eleven years. It was work I enjoyed but in a very stressful environment. Although I would miss it, it was a relief to move on.

In late November, we moved in with my mom and dad, but our new house was nowhere near finished. God's timing is always perfect and just what we need. However, hindsight is sometimes necessary to see it.

Mom wasn't doing well. Mom and I had talked and prayed together daily for years, and our families had always visited on Sundays after church several times a month. She seemed fine for those brief visits. Although my husband, Tony, had expressed some concern, I had never seen it coming. This was Mom, the one who was always there. Now the cancer was back.

My sweet dog, Tippy, died in January. My mom went home to be with the Lord in February. Her funeral was a grand celebration of her loving and generous life. Even today, twelve years later, I meet people who tell me about things my mom had done for them out of her generous heart. The pastors at her funeral were men she had prayed into the kingdom.

Caring for my mother in her last months was one of God's most gracious gifts to me. It was the hardest thing I have ever done, but one of my life's treasures. Unless you've been there, it's hard to understand. I still miss her and her unfailing, deep relationship with Jesus.

We had moved into our new house in April on Easter Sunday. The workmen continued finishing things until May 30. I remember the day because my oldest son's wedding rehearsal dinner was held in our new home that evening! I was almost convinced the builder and his men were going to actually live with us.

The year continued to be very stressful. I heard my youngest son say, "Uh, Mom! (pause) ... My girlfriend's pregnant." Then our middle son married and ill-advisedly we were sure at the time.

But hindsight is a wonderful thing. Now we can see God's hand clearly, even if some of the paths seemed convoluted at the time. We have three of the most beautiful, loving, godly daughters-in-law imaginable, six grandchildren and one on the way. Most importantly, we have the assurance of our loved ones' relationship with Jesus—their future is sure.

I've learned through life that God's plans are often hidden in packages of circumstances we don't appreciate at the time, the purpose only revealed later. As I look back, I see how badly my faith faltered during some of those times, and the consequences that lack of faith created as I tried to work things out my own way. Trusting God in these seemingly adverse circumstances would have given a much happier result much sooner with so much less grief.

"When do you think God's gonna let me go home to be with Mama?" my Dad asked.

"When He's ready, Dad," was all I could say. I took another bite of the apple pie and looked up just in time to see him falling over from his chair at the kitchen table. I caught him before he got to the floor and cried out for Tony to come and help. Dad had gone to be with Mama and Jesus. In retrospect, I could see it ready to happen. He had worked hard since Mama's death ten months earlier to straighten things out in his life and home. She had told him before she died, "You're not going to die until you've given your life to Jesus!" He made sure he did first thing with a call to mom's pastor shortly after her death. Then God showed him about relationships that needed healing, and he also worked hard to get things at the old homestead cleaned out and ready. He had moved in with us just ten days before, after it had become too precarious to navigate the stairs in his home. He was a sweet and gentle man. I still miss him, too.

We've been in our new home twelve years now and still love it. Retirement is good! Our plan was to be here to take care of Mom and Dad, but they were both gone within the first year. However, God's purposes didn't end there. After a few years, He led me to SCSM through a chance meeting with Chaplain Liz at our church, and I've been committed ever since. I had trained myself for years on the computer and taken classes in high-end graphic arts packages, using the skills in creating realtor and business association newsletters, flyers, directories and for other volunteer work. I loved it! Now I'm able to enjoy using these skills again for an organization I know is making a difference.

A Gift Beyond Measure

Frankie Schuman

Whoa! What did Dad just say? Enough daydreaming, it was time for me to pay attention, remain focused on here and now. My sisters and I were given fair warning about this meeting. With three teenage daughters, Dad knew better than to try and pull off a family meeting on a Friday evening without *strategic* planning. Gathered around the dining room table with my parents and sisters, my thoughts began to wander again.

Typical teenagers, we seemed to take turns getting into hot water for breaking curfew or some other house rule. Did the three of us commit a serious offense on the very same day? No, Dad looked much too relaxed and upbeat to be doling out punishment, and Mom was so bright-eyed and cheerful.

Dad was bursting with excitement. His voice escalating, the words tumbled and tripped from his mouth. Focused now, I heard praise for our country and, "I hope someday my three girls will get to see the world, but before you do, I want you to see the United States of America and love and appreciate our country." That was the bottom line.

Dad was planning an eight week cross-country excursion with his wife and teenage daughters. Was he crazy or a saint? Maybe a crazy saint! We piled into Dad's 1960 white Bonneville on June 30 to begin an adventure that would end just short of the first day of school. Was I filled with excitement or gratitude for this road trip? Not a bit. I was fifteen years old and felt robbed. All I could think about was how this trip was about to mess up my summer vacation.

Dad had no need to remind us of his love for the USA. Independence Day ranked a notch below Christmas in our family. Dad transformed from Pat Villani into Uncle Sam each year on the Fourth of July. Thinking about it made me smile. Then memories of *his story* flooded over me, bringing a familiar pang to my heart. It is the story that fueled his patriotism and fanned his overwhelming desire to share a tour of "America the Beautiful" with his family.

Dad grew up to be tall, dark and handsome, a real heartthrob. A high school football star, he dreamed of becoming a history teacher and football coach. Bright and talented, his hard-won scholarship could help make his dream come true. World War 2 shattered that dream.

His maturity, intelligence and quick-wit did not go unnoticed in the Army. In a blink he was promoted to Sergeant and soon Acting Captain of his platoon. One beautiful, sunny morning as he took respite from battle beneath the cool shade of an olive tree, a land mine exploded. He lost his helmet and a good portion of his head. As he lay bleeding, he could hear but not see or move. In the distance he heard a voice shout, "Pat's dead, leave him, go! *Run, Now!*" But one of his men, a courageous and compassionate soldier, refused to leave him and miraculously carried him from the line of fire to safety.

He endured the pain and agony of several brain surgeries. A titanium plate was implanted in his head to replace missing pieces of his skull. Thanks to God, medical heroics and a very brave fellow soldier, Dad's recovery is a testimony of love, hope, compassion and strength. Following months of rehabilitation, he triumphed over adversity, vowing to return to the spot where he was wounded and Uncle Frank, my mother's brother who also was Dad's best friend and my namesake, was killed in battle.

That vow was fulfilled in 1995. He returned to that fateful spot in Italy at the age of 78 with his beloved wife, my mother Louise. My Dad, commended with the Purple Heart Award, died on January 11, 2003. I love how he appreciated the simple things in life and how our family can treasure his legacy of love, faith, hope and courage. I can feel his love, see his smile, hear his laughter and will always cherish his memory.

What about that family road trip? Together we toured 46 magnificent states. It truly was a gift beyond measure. I learned firsthand that America *is* beautiful, from *sea-to-shining-sea*. God bless America, land of the free, home of the brave, and the countless individuals willing to sacrifice all to defend and protect our great nation!

> Guard my life, for I am faithful to you;
> save your servant who trusts in you.
> You are my God; have mercy on me, Lord,
> for I call to you all day long.
> Bring joy to your servant, Lord,
> for I put my trust in you.
> You, Lord, are forgiving and good,
> abounding in love to all who call to you.
> Hear my prayer, Lord; listen to my cry for mercy.
> When I am in distress, I call to you, because you answer
> me. (NIV, Psalm 86:2-7)

Remembering With Tea

Sharon Mamatai Khosa

My name is Sharon Khosa. I met Chaplain Liz Danielsen through the SCSM Grief Group. I had experienced back-to-back losses of my mother, Agnes Mhlanga, and my younger brother, Arnold Mhlanga, who died two years apart from violent car accidents. Two years later my elder brother, Theod Mhlanga, was involved in a car accident which left him paralyzed from the waist down. These experiences left me frozen with a fear of driving. I kept thinking that my family was possibly cursed. I literally died with my mom. I had no zeal for life. I was just bitter.

I attended Liz's sessions on grief and learned a lot about myself and how to go on a healing journey from loss. Liz taught me not to die with my mom and my brother. She challenged me to find a purpose for my loved ones' deaths. I prayed and fasted for a long time, and the Lord took away the spirit of fear of driving and replaced it with peace. This was my biggest spiritual breakthrough ever. My mind was also renewed, and I started looking at life differently.

My mom had been a fervent prayer warrior all her life, so I decided to continue her legacy of prayer in my family and with other people. To honor her life, I decided to hold an annual tea party for ladies on my birthday and share the day with other mothers—drinking from them and pouring out part of myself to others. My mother had always loved tea and many of her teaching moments were spent over a hot cup of tea. Her passion for people, prayer and tea lives on through these tea parties.

During the tea party we have a lot of moments where the ladies speak into each other's lives. We have a Teacup Personality Check. I have each woman bring one tea cup. I mix them up and each takes a different cup. I encourage the ladies to positively describe the woman behind the cup, and it is surprising how right they have been. We also have a Remembrance Bouquet. I ask if anyone wants to share about a loss they have experienced by picking a flower from a bunch and sharing what that person taught them. Together we take a painful bouquet mingled with loss, hurt, and bitterness and end with a beautiful masterpiece. This is very healing. The bouquet is presented to whoever had the most recent loss. The ladies love this! I learned about this activity in one of the Grief Group classes.

I also went on a quest to discover why my parents had given me the names I have. I discovered I am the daughter of the Rose of Sharon Jesus Christ, so I must have the aroma of a flower and be sweet, fresh and delicate. My middle name is Namatayi, an African name which means "the prayerful one." Wow! I had discovered my purpose and mission for life.

I am still on the journey to healing thanks to Spiritual Care Support Ministries. They do follow-up care by inviting me to refresher seminars and sharing with others over breakfasts, luncheons, and at sleepovers and picnics. Now I am excited, passionate, and alive! I feel I am truly blessed! Praise the Lord!

Celebrating a Special Birthday

Betty Reedy

Saturday, July 18, 2009, dawned as a clear, comfortable day with a gentle breeze blowing. This special day would have been the eighty-fifth birthday for my dear husband, Elmer Mason Reedy. We always celebrated birthdays as the celebrant wished (e.g., how was that day to be remembered, what kind of cake was to be baked, which restaurant would be the choice of location for dinner, would this be the year for a party, would we visit family/friends, etc.).

I was in a quandary as to how I was going to remember this day since I would be on my own to commemorate a day that was not my special day. But I wanted to do something very special because of the milestone birthday.

My plan of action came to light early that morning. I had hoped that the hydrangeas that had been planted eighteen years ago would still be fresh enough in bloom so I could take a large bouquet to be placed lovingly on Elmer's gravesite. He was very proud of those plants that God helped him nurture over the years.

My wish had been granted. Early in the morning I picked a beautiful bunch of flowers, wrapped them with wet paper towels and headed to Stonewall Memory Gardens. On arrival I placed them in the vase and talked to him for a few minutes, reminding him of our past celebrations. I then walked over to a bench that was nearby, sat down and let my mind start to wander. It was peaceful and for the most part quiet. A gentle breeze would blow every once in a while. I sat there in my own thoughts thinking about our fifty-six years of togetherness, or as some of our friends had mentioned over the years, my being his shadow and him being mine. We always did things together. There were lots of memories.

After about forty-five minutes and many shed tears, I decided that it was time to leave that hollowed spot on God's green earth. I walked back up to the site and bid Elmer a happy eighty-fifth birthday and told him that I was going home to make a German chocolate cake, his very favorite that he always requested. I was going to eat the first piece and *enjoy* it. I did just that! That cake was the best one I had made in years, and I *did* enjoy that first piece. I then shared with neighbors and friends.

The day turned out to be a different kind of remembrance. However, I felt that I had celebrated in the direction that God had guided for me that day.

Wearing the Other Shoes

Amy Furr

I'm used to wearing these shoes, so to speak. They were inexpensive and I've had them for years. They are comfortable, broken in, fit well, and I know what to expect (as much as one can know what to expect in a crisis or disaster response).

Recently, however, I have had to wear different shoes. My beloved grandfather died several weeks ago. Even though I know all the steps to grieving, and therefore, should know what to expect, each day has brought new surprises for me. These new shoes aren't comfortable. They don't fit properly, have unwanted holes, and are awkward. They were expensive, too, including the cost of my grandfather's life and now, my health. I'm used to taking care of everyone else, not the one being taken care of. One day I'm fine, the next day I can't get off the couch, or I am breaking down in the middle of the grocery store while my toddler watches me. While I know this is normal, it doesn't feel normal. It's not *my* normal. It's not me. *These aren't my shoes.* With the grief has come an explosion of pain inside my body, a reaction to the stress. Between the grief and the pain, not only can I not function, I don't want to function. I know this is normal. It's my *new* normal, but I don't like wearing these shoes. They belong to someone else. *Don't they?*

My grandfather died on a Wednesday. I usually go to "work" at SCSM on Thursdays. There was no question that I was going to go to work. Where else was I going to go? What else was I supposed to do? I kept baking and cooking everything I could get my hands on in the kitchen all day Wednesday. At midnight, completely baked-out, exhausted and grieving, I looked around thinking, "What now? Oh, I should go to bed now so I can be fresh in the morning for work, right? Right." Of course, I didn't sleep and I ran late that morning. I like to be at work by 9:15AM to be ready when the café opens at 10AM, but it was almost 10AM before I even pulled out of my own driveway for the twenty-five minute drive. I found out along the way that my son's daycare was closed due to the public schools having only a half-day. Great! Now I was going to have both kids with me. This would be interesting! Even if I had known ahead of time that his daycare was closed, I still would have gone to the center. Again, where else was I going to go? What else was I supposed to do? While setting up the food, the rest of the staff came down for our morning hugs and to express their condolences. Several of them said they were surprised to see me. Where else was I going to go? What else was I supposed to do? This is where I belong and needed to be. This is where *my* healing has always begun and where I knew it would begin again.

Wearing the other shoes isn't so bad. My toes are a bit pinched. I have slipped and fallen a few times, and I know I will again before all is said and done. But, now that I've read the shoebox and had the training, I know a little bit about what to expect. I'm also in the care of great, loving people who know what to expect and how to guide me while I wear these shoes. My grandfather will always be dear to my family, so I don't think I will ever be fully finished with these new shoes. I just hope to have a few good days in between when I can wear my old ones.

A Place of Peace

Beverly Ruane

"God is great, but sometimes life ain't good. When I pray, it doesn't always turn out like I think it should." These are words from the song, *Anyway,* sung by Martina McBride. That's exactly the way it seems to be. Life isn't always fair, but we need to remember that God is always in charge.

My life was normal prior to April 29, 2002. I worked, took care of my grandson, my family, and anything that was a day-to-day activity. That night my life became anything but normal. My eighteen year old son, Matthew, was shot and killed in front of our home by a random act of violence. I felt as if my life had ended.

I was in a fog during the first year without Matthew. At times I felt I was inside a bubble, looking out into the world without being able to touch it. I didn't believe Matthew was gone. Every day I would stand at the door and look for him to come walking up the street. I was angry at Matthew for leaving me and at God for taking him from me. I was mostly angry at the men who killed him. The emotion I felt most was guilt. As a mother, I didn't protect my child. I felt it was my fault he was killed. I felt guilty for being angry at Matthew and God. I even felt guilty for feeling guilty.

Completely consumed by my grief, all I could think about was Matthew and how I was supposed to live the rest of my life without him. I had other family and friends who needed me but somehow that didn't seem to make a difference. Every day, every minute I would relive the moment I heard he had been shot, seeing and touching his calm but lifeless face. I tried to find answers and console myself in any way possible.

To help, I began to read every book I could find on grief and the death of a child. As I read, I was surprised to see that those parents felt the same way I did. It was as if I had written those books. I began to write in a journal. It is a place you can write whatever you are feeling and thinking in any way you want. It doesn't matter if it makes any sense, it's only for you, and you will understand it. I began to go to a bereaved parents group. Talking and listening to other bereaved parents helped me. They understood exactly what I was going through.

Another group I attended was the SCSM Grief Group. There God sent a wonderful couple who had also lost their son to murder. It was at Grief Group that things seem to click. I understood why I felt the way I did and that it was okay. I understood the continuous roller coaster ride. The same emotions applied to me as others yet were also unique to me. I prayed every day that God would see me through the death of my son.

Another comfort for me was gardening which I have always enjoyed. Planning and planting varieties of plants and flowers always brought me joy. After Matthew died, even the joy of gardening left me. I didn't enjoy doing anything I had previously taken pleasure in doing. Matthew died in April, the beginning of spring with new life. I felt such despair. New life was beginning, yet my son was dead.

I would plant so many different flowers that my yard had always been the prettiest and most colorful on the block. Every time I came home with more plants, my neighbors would ask me where I would plant those. I would always find a spot! With the loss of my son, gardening didn't matter anymore. So what if I had a pretty yard full of flowers. I didn't have my son.

After two or three weeks, I finally decided to venture outside and make an attempt at planting flowers. My heart was not in it at all. The joy I once had every time I gardened was no longer there. I made myself garden because if I didn't, I may never do it again. I began to dig in the soil to prepare it for planting. I dug and dug. Then I began to dig harder. Each time I applied more force until at times I was actually beating the ground. I discovered what wonderful therapy gardening offered. I could dig and beat the ground as hard as I wanted to, and it wouldn't get hurt or fight back. The ground was very forgiving.

While we were out of town burying my son in a beautiful place on top of a hill in the Blue Ridge Mountains overlooking a valley, my friend and neighbor created a small memorial garden for me. Before I began working in the yard, I would sit in the chair outside, read and write, and look at the small area which came to be known as "Matthew's Garden."

Before the summer was over, I once again began to enjoy gardening. It was relaxing and a release. The more I gardened and cared for "Matthew's Garden," the more I wanted a large memorial garden where I could go, sit, and meditate. A peaceful place I could go and think about Matthew and my life.

With those thoughts I began to create a memorial garden in my mind. Everywhere I went I looked to see if there was a place for one. Whenever I visited a nursery, I looked at the various plants and pictured them in the garden I had created in my mind. I became passionate about my dream. I never gave up hope, yet I wondered how it would ever happen. Where would the money come from? Not only would the land need to be purchased but so would all the plants and flowers, in addition to the construction.

One night I attended a Master Gardeners meeting. One of the topics discussed was the creation of gardens called "Place of Peace." I was very excited and after the meeting approached the landscape designer, Ron Cloer, asking if it would be possible to have an area to create a memorial garden for our children on behalf of The Bereaved Parents of the USA. His response was, "Absolutely!"

That was the beginning of the reality of my dream. Not only was the land being donated for use by the Benedictine Sisters, Ron Cloer offered to create the design for the garden free of charge.

The only thing we needed was to raise money for the plants and construction. The construction of the memorial garden began on a cold and windy day in late December 2006. Another bereaved mother and father, my youngest daughter, and I planted twelve bushes, followed by four trees the next day. It was the physical start of a dream come true.

The garden is on the campus of the Benedictine Monastery where Linton Hall School is located, on Linton Hall Road in Bristow, Virginia. The construction of all the gardens being created will take several years. It will be called "Place of Peace" and offer areas for people to go, relax, and meditate.

This memorial garden for our children will be a place parents and family may go for many years to walk around, sit, enjoy, and reflect on our children.

A Precious Gift

Brenda Rector

On October 7, 2011, I lost the most precious gift I have ever received in my life. She was my beautiful daughter, Jacinda, whom I adored more than anything in this world. I say the word "gift" because I adopted Jacinda.

Jacinda came into my life when she was nine months old. She was returned to her family by the Department of Social Services after I had her in foster care for nearly a year. After being with her biological family for nine months, they decided as a family to give her back to me. They saw the bond that we had after I continued to travel to her home and visit her when she was with her family in Maryland. So, when I was given custody of her by her family, I knew that God wanted us to be together. This is why I know Jacinda was a gift from God to me! This is when I decided to officially adopt her. Her adoption was finalized when she was three years old.

Jacinda was nine years old when she suddenly died. The cause of death has not yet been determined. When I first heard she had passed away, my heart was in pain that I could not explain. I first kept wondering and asking God, "Why?" Why would He give me my daughter that I had prayed for and then take her away from me at the age of nine?

Thank God for wonderful co-workers! They immediately stepped in and took over to assist me in everything I needed to do. I work at West Gate Elementary school in Prince William County. They went far beyond the call of duty to be there for me. Even co-workers whom I used to work with and have since gone to different schools helped. They were all so awesome! God puts people in your life for a reason, and I thank Him for the people I am blessed to know.

Since going to Spiritual Care Support Ministries, I started to see that I was not the only one who was experiencing the hurt of losing a young one. I realized that there were so many stories worse than mine. So many times we forget that there's *always* someone worse off than we are. I just thank God that she did not suffer with sickness. I am grateful that I never once had to see her in pain. I realized that God had just loaned me my gift for a while, and I understand that some people wish they had nine years when they've had less.

I continue to walk in faith and accept the things I cannot change. My faith is getting stronger. Words can never express the feelings of hurt, but through it all, I know God is in charge. I have good and bad days, but through it all, I will continue to "enter His gates with thanksgiving and his courts with praise; give thanks to Him and praise His name" (Psalm 100:4).

If I could say one thing to people in the world, it would be that through all of your good and bad experiences in life, always remember that there's someone worse off than you. Lean and depend on God to be your refuge in the time of a storm. He is truly an on-time God. Yes, He is!

A Testimony of Grief

Dee

It will soon be two years since I lost my darling husband. It was during the Christmas season. As my daughter, Brenda, and I entered the funeral home to make final arrangements, I couldn't help but notice the large beautifully decorated Christmas tree. I just "lost it." I remember thinking, "Why do they have to acerbate my sorrow by reminding me that Christmas will never be the same again." I had lost my mother just a few weeks before my husband. At a time like this, one's emotions can run amok. Mine ranged from unbelief and denial that my Rod was gone, to utter helplessness. I really needed to talk about these feelings with someone but all I could do was cry. I couldn't even pray.

My pastors and many others encouraged me to join the SCSM Grief Group, but I just could not imagine sharing my grief with strangers. A few months later I decided to give it a try. Brenda came with me, bless her heart!

That first night on the way to the meeting I was okay until I entered the room. I could feel the tears building up. Chaplain Liz had asked each of us if we would introduce ourselves and if we chose to, briefly tell our reason for being there. When it was my turn I couldn't even squeak out my name. The tears flowed uncontrollably the rest of the session.

My husband's death left me feeling like less than half a person, and the part that was left was shattered into tiny pieces. I felt that I would never recover.

Grief Group was a real jump-start on my way to healing. I also had a wonderful support system—my family (especially my daughter, Brenda), my Sunday School class, friends, church, and my faith.

As I continued with the SCSM Grief Group, I gained strength from hearing how others were coping and also listening to the wise and comforting words of our leaders. The videos helped a great deal as well. It seems that no matter how devastating one's situation may be, you always find someone else who has had it worse than you.

During the months that followed the loss of my mother and husband, I also lost three friends, two cousins, and my dear step mom. I decided to go through Grief Group again.

I was amazed at how strong I had become. This time I could actually participate in the discussions.

God knows our innermost feelings and offers hope and help. We are really not alone. God surrounds us with special people who help us meet the challenges we encounter. Jesus knows our sorrow. Jesus wept when He saw the pain His friends were experiencing. Those two simple words, "Jesus wept," are full of rich heartfelt meaning. It is comforting to know that our Savior has such a tender heart. When we are at our lowest, Christ sits with us, holds us, and weeps with us.

My first winter without Rod, I fluctuated between unbelief and brutal reality. The days and nights seemed endless. Each morning when I woke up to this eerily quiet house, after only two or three hours of sleep, I would say to myself, "This is going to be the rest of my life." I worried that people would forget all about this wonderful man I had lost.

I couldn't keep my mind on reading so I tried working crossword puzzles and Sudoku. It helped to pass the time. I prayed, watched movies, ate chocolate, played music, ate chocolate, talked with friends on the phone, and ate more chocolate. I gained twenty pounds in a short period of time. Somehow I got through the long, cold winter.

A year passed and it was Christmas again. I did not put up our tree. I tried, but I just couldn't do it. Chaplain Liz said it was okay.

As this winter passed and I could concentrate more on my Bible reading, I began to feel the Lord's presence more and more. Until now, I had not eaten at our breakfast table. It was just too difficult. Rod was not sitting across from me. My diet was a disaster, which included chips, the ever necessary chocolate, peanut butter, and cereal.

Spring finally came! I had been praying continually that God would lift this constant underlying sadness. One morning I woke up and for the first time had the desire for coffee, bacon, and eggs. I rather light-heartedly prepared them and sat down at our breakfast table for the first time since Rod had been gone. While eating, I suddenly heard birds singing very loudly! Now, we have gazillions of birds every spring, but until that moment, I had not heard them sing or was even aware of their presence.

I praised the Lord! It seemed like my answer to prayer and a promise that I would be happy again. Perhaps not like before, but happy nonetheless.

I would like to mention some things that really helped me. It may be different for you as we all cope differently.

- No one wants to hear this, but regular exercise may help you feel better about yourself and your situation.
- Keep a journal of your thoughts and feelings. Keeping this on a regular basis can prove to be a comfort when looking back later. You can see your rate of healing even though you don't realize it at the time. This was one of the greatest tools for me.
- Look for and spend time with friends. It's okay to need and depend on friends and family, especially during times of loneliness.
- Accept your loneliness. Most of the time we want to run from difficulty. The challenge is to understand and accept that

loneliness. It will teach us more about who we are and who we are becoming. We can learn from this uncomfortable invader.

- Try not to make important decisions, if possible.
- Try not to make changes too soon. I would not remove Rod's Bible from the kitchen table where he had left it that last Sunday he taught his class. I finally moved it to our bedroom this summer.
- I slept with his robe for a year and a half.
- To keep from being afraid at night, I relied on Psalm 4:8 that says, "In peace I will lie down and sleep, for you alone, LORD, make me dwell in safety."
- Just remember that even though you are grieving, Christmas can still be a special season of faith and a time of prayer both individually and with others.

I hope you have the courage to attend a Grief Group. If you receive even half the help and encouragement I received, you will be truly blessed.

Remember, God has a plan for your life. Be open to it and let Him work it out in His time. Just remember, no matter how dark the tunnel, a light will appear, probably when you least expect it. It did for me.

Teens and Grief

Gina

On September 6, 2005, my sons, John and James, lost their dad. He died suddenly of a heart attack at forty-two years old. John had been living with his dad before he died, while James lived with my husband, his stepbrothers, and me. After his father's death, John had to transfer to a new school, make new friends, and re-adjust to a large family life full-time. At his dad's house, he was an only child. John was overwhelmed with grief and frequently told me how much he hated me. He couldn't yet see that being at home with us was just where he needed to be.

James did not have the bond that John did with their father. He always felt closer to his stepfather. He felt anger for missing out on time with his dad and struggled to grasp onto memories of him. John's grieving was more outward and James' was more inward with occasional bursts of crying and questions.

Our pastor suggested grief counseling at Spiritual Care Support Ministries. I set up an appointment to meet Chaplain Liz or as we call her, Ms. Liz. She spoke with the boys and me about the things we were feeling. She reassured us this was normal. She spoke with the boys individually also. Then at the end of the session she prayed with us. We began seeing Ms. Liz weekly and all looked forward to seeing her. The boys would always share what was on their hearts with her, and they learned to grieve and grow.

Ms. Liz would generously offer me reading material. It was through reading one of these booklets that I learned about a beautiful word, *empathy*. I realized that I had to grieve for my ex-husband, something I was resisting, forgive him, and let go of all the bitterness I felt. Otherwise, I would not be able to help my sons grieve. In doing so, I could be there for them, listen when they wanted to talk, help them relive memories and things about their dad, focus on good things about him, and plan a road trip to put flowers on his grave.

John and James are now happy boys at eleven and sixteen years of age. They are both open to talking about their dad's death. I believe grief counseling at SCSM helped them to feel confident and not ashamed. In December, we honored the boys and their father with three lights on the SCSM Christmas tree. It was a great time to reflect on how far they've come, how much SCSM and Ms. Liz had helped us, and how good God is.

Whose Plan Is This Anyway?

Susan R. Izzie

I think many of us are under the misconception that we are in control of our lives. I had mine planned and things were going exactly the way I thought they should. I had married my soul mate, and had two children, including a girl and a boy. I lived in a place I loved, in a house I loved, and I had my parents living right down the hill. I had a job that I adored where I had the privilege of working around children every day. It helped relieve some of the stress of having my own children leave the nest. We were also blessed to be a part of the Novum Church family. They have supported us in every way possible through prayer and encouragement in our times of need.

We moved to Virginia from Maryland to be closer to my parents as they aged. It was a perfect set-up. We helped them and they helped us. We spent a lot of time together just enjoying each other's company. They blessed us every day, and we planned to take care of them in their old age.

I found my identity in being a wife and mother. My two children had gone away to college and seemed very happy. My husband and I were getting to spend more time together, and life was exactly what I thought it should be. I have chronic illness and pain and all too often find myself in an operating room. This was not a new situation and my family coped with these hurdles well.

Then it seemed that my plans started unraveling. Our son was arrested and sentenced to ten years in federal prison. How did this happen? He is a caring, joyous person, but drugs had pulled him into a dark, uncaring world. I could no longer protect him from the harsh realities of his choices. I could no longer protect myself or my family from the pain. I was adjusting the best I could to a devastating situation for our entire family. I am very close to our two children. I had my husband to lean on and my parents to help us through. I had to give up the job I loved since I was no longer able to concentrate on anything that required a lot of my energy.

On May 24, 2008, a neighbor called to say my parents had been in a minor accident about a half mile from our house and were asking for me. I arrived at the scene of the accident to find them both coherent, although my mother had obviously broken her femur. Due to the suspicion of internal bleeding, my mother was taken to UVA in a helicopter, and I went with my father in the ambulance. When we arrived at the hospital, my mother was in trauma surgery. I would never see her conscious again. Two days later, my father was also in a coma from bleeding in the brain on one side of his head and a clot on the other. There was no hope for either of them. I found medical directives appointing me as the person that makes the final decisions about life support in dire medical situations. I had to choose to let them both go together. This is a choice I don't wish on anyone. It is the most difficult decision I have ever had to make, and I was only able to do so with the help of God. We had one funeral with two people to lay at rest. Two of the people I loved the most in this world were suddenly taken from me. I had been prepared to take care of them but not to lose them. They were living in Glory with God. I was living a nightmare.

I felt that my whole world was caving in around me. After being rolled in to surgery for the thirteenth time, I did not feel I could cope with the cycle of pain emotionally or physically any longer. What had happened to my plans for happiness and relaxation? When it was suggested by a friend that I seek help at Spiritual Care Support Ministries, I was not only at the bottom of the well, but it was an arid and dark place. I was reluctant to seek help since I thought no one could help me. I was too far in my world of depression to even care what happened next.

Chaplain Liz was gracious enough to provide one-on-one counseling since I was unable to be around people. I was convinced that there was no way she could reach me in the depths of my devastation but knew I had nowhere else to turn. Over time she has been able to put in to perspective for me that no matter what the circumstances, we are to find joy in Christ. This is GOD's plan, not mine. What made me think I was in control anyway? God is there in the depths of our pain, and He loves us so much and wants us to trust Him in all circumstances. Chaplain Liz was able to convince me of the benefits of a Grief Group. I wasn't interested at first but once I was there, I found much comfort in others.

I no longer think I have the perfect plan. God has the perfect plan. There are reasons for every scenario He sends our way, and we need to trust in His love and believe that He will take care of us.

Is the pain and sadness gone? Not yet, but with the love of God and the guidance of Spiritual Care Support Ministries, I am on my way to healing. I am no longer languishing in the bottom of the well but have started the long voyage to the surface to find joy.

Nono

Vito DiIenna

May 1 is a significant day for me. May 1, 2008, marks the one year anniversary of my Nono Vito's passing (nono, properly spelled nonno, is Italian for grandfather). Nono left this world on my father's birthday. I lost my dad only two years earlier in December 2005, and for some reason, today, May 1, is the first day I have developed the courage to write this piece.

In June 2005, my family was struggling after the recent loss of my infant cousin, Dillon. Losing Dad in December was all too much for us to handle. I was twenty-one at the time and felt like my world was imploding. I was trying to deal with the pain and grief of death, finish up college, get a job, and think of what I would be doing for the rest of my life. Even though it is best to not make any major decisions after the loss of anyone close to you, sometimes life cannot wait. Somehow, through the support of my family and friends, I was able to finish school. I now find myself a Virginian (at least for the moment).

Life has been unbearably difficult without all my loved ones. It often feels like there is a hole in the middle of me that I cannot seem to plug. I pick up the phone to ask Dad about how I change out the exhaust manifold on my '93 Mercury Tracer, only to remember I will have to answer those questions without him now. It is simply a natural inclination that I will never get over.

People say that as time goes on, you should get over the loss. I think that is complete nonsense. There is no such thing as forgetting the pain or covering it up. Grief is truly the untamable rollercoaster of life. I was having so many problems dealing with my pain and grief that I reached out and decided to attend a grief support group.

I often donate some of my extra money to a charity or cause I think is working to make this world better. My company, ExxonMobil, has a program that contributes additional money to a charity if you donate. I decided to attend the charity fair. Walking through the aisles and aisles of charities, I came across Spiritual Care Support Ministries and it sounded interesting. I thought, "What do they do? Heal your pain by healing your spirit?" It sounded a bit too otherworldly for me, but I give almost anything a chance. I began speaking to Joe Toth who explained that the group works to help bereaved people who are grieving. I thought it sounded like a good cause to which I would donate. I began to walk away from the table, but I turned around and asked if it would be okay if I attended. I explained I was having trouble getting on with life since losing Dad, and I could use some help. Joe's reaction was so positive that I could not help but attend. He had me feeling a little better right there at the booth.

The courage I had that day to ask if I could attend was one of the best decisions I have made to help myself. The SCSM support group has been a remarkable inspiration for me. Liz, Sue and Joe have been a group that I look to not only for support, but as a role model during those extremely tough times. When I have those really bad days, I think back to the discussions I had in the support group and I often ask myself, "What would they do in this situation?"

One of my biggest problems before attending the support group was the feeling of being alone. I knew that my family and I were experiencing the same feelings, but what about the rest of the world? Haven't other people lost family members? Don't other people start crying out of nowhere or miss their train stops because they are so distracted? These are the questions I continuously asked myself. Not until I attended the support group did I really have the opportunity to share in the feelings of others and realize that I am not alone in this struggle that we call life.

Liz and the support group attendees have created an atmosphere that makes me comfortable so I am able to open up and share my true feelings. An added bonus is the good friends I have made, especially the Gays. The Gay family recently lost a son around my age. I know we struggle through our pain together, but being together lets me express my emotions. Often men have a difficult time expressing their feelings because they are not expected to show emotion, but you put my friend, Tom, and me in a room, and there is no problem expressing our feelings. We probably sound like my Granny and her ladies.

Before attending the support group, I had a very difficult time looking at any pictures or being reminded of what life was like before losing those I loved so much. It was difficult for me to remember the good parts of the life I shared with my family. However, now I can look at pictures and although I still shed tears sometimes, I can smile. I think of and am thankful for the great memories of the times we shared together.

One of the best memories I have with my father is at Coney Island Amusement Park. I was supposed to be in school for the day, but I asked Dad if we could go spend some time together. He took me out of school, took the day off from work, and we went (which is probably, by the way, a heinous crime by today's standards). It was the best time I can remember the two of us having. There were no lines and hotdogs all day. I even think we rode the Cyclone Rollercoaster a record seven times in a row.

I am now in the second grief support group, feeling that I am making progress every day. That does not mean that I do not have my fair share of upsetting and bad days. Sometimes I find myself shedding tears because I see, smell, or hear reminders of those whom I have lost. That hole inside me I described earlier has not gone away, but I have learned to live with that hole. It is almost as if it has become a part of who I am.

My words cannot express how thankful I am to be a part of Spiritual Care Support Ministries. I feel that I am at home when we have our weekly sessions. Liz, being a fellow Brooklynite, does remind me a bit of my real home—New York. They have helped me to view life in a different light, not feel guilty for living, and make the most of the rest of my life because this is what the ones I lost would have wanted.

My stepbrother used to say Dad was just too good for this world, and I think he is right. We will never understand some things, nor should we try to, because they simply do not make sense. Our family will be forever changed, and the lives of the people whom he touched will be as well.

Some moments have an amazing intangible quality, a sense that is indescribable by words. I think of them now, and the thought of the three of them together brings both contentment and pain. As I write, I definitely have a feeling that everyone I have lost, including Dillon, Dad, and Nono are looking down on me. I love you guys and miss you.

You Give and Take Away

Caitlyn Hammarberg

Time flies. You could be sitting counting the seconds that are going by, thinking time is standing still. Then the next moment, you are looking back and wondering where the last nine years have gone. Nine years. One year away from a whole decade. At eleven years old, my life drastically changed. I wasn't supposed to lose one of my parents at such a young age. That wasn't how life was supposed to happen. I went from one day being the happiest child with a full family to a grieving one with the head of the household missing. He was our support, our anchor, the one that kept us all together. God took that away.

> You give and take away
> You give and take away
> My heart will choose to say
> Lord, blessed be your name
> (Redman, "Blessed Be Your Name")

What happened next was not by my own strength but God's. I could have turned against God, I could have run away from my family, or I could have turned to something or someone to satisfy my needs.

What happened next was my choice.

And I chose God.

I chose the One that I will never completely understand. I chose the One that has different plans than my own.

But I also chose the One who knows my name. I chose the One that makes everything good in His timing. I chose the One who will give me everlasting life, joy, and satisfaction.

This life-changing moment in my life, losing my father, was a blessing in disguise. Looking back, I wouldn't have changed anything. If I had a choice of having my life as it is now or having my dad, I would choose the pain all over again. It might sound crazy, but that pain brought me to the relationship I have with God now. It's not perfect. I make mistakes and at times I even deny God, but God *always* takes me back. As far as I run, I can never out run God.

CHAPTER 2

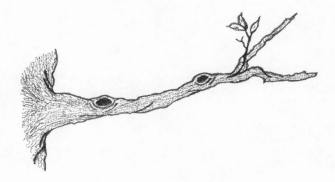

The Unhealthy Limbs

The unhealthy limbs of the tree are unable to maintain their growth and begin healing without relying on the nourishment of the trunk and, frequently, the support of other branches. There are those among us who must rely on the strength of God and the support of fellow Christians to manage a life of chronic illness.

Chronic illness will sap your strength and your hope. God asks that we care for those who cannot care for themselves. These stories describe the suffering of chronic illness and pain, and help us understand the coping skills required to live in a world of daily physical challenges. Reliance on God makes the difference between thriving or just surviving.

From Pain to Purpose

Mary J. Yerkes

"I'm afraid there is no cure. We can only treat the symptoms," Dr. Price explained, almost apologetically.

Speechless, I lingered over her words struggling to grasp the implications of the diagnosis—rheumatoid arthritis. A systemic disease causing inflammation in the joints, the inflammatory cells slowly digest bone and cartilage. The result is pain, loss of movement and deformity. My body was attacking itself!

I had been living with pain and swelling for several months. Yet, the diagnosis blindsided me.

"Maybe the test results aren't mine. They could have gotten confused with someone else's, right?" Pleading, I searched her eyes hoping to find some acknowledgement that this might be true. She only shook her head.

I drove home, hot tears spilling down my cheeks.

Facing the Losses

As the disease progressed, simple, everyday tasks grew increasingly difficult. Morning was the hardest. I dreaded taking that first step out of bed each morning. Gingerly, I would dangle one foot over the edge of the bed, testing the intensity of the pain by slowing putting weight on one foot then the other. Stiffly, I would shuffle to the bathroom, looking decades older than my thirty-eight years.

As I made my way through the day, my thoughts would often turn towards my aunt, crippled from her early thirties by the same disease. One image, in particular, was difficult to shake. In the morning, my uncle would lean over her feet as she sat on the edge of the bed helping her put on her shoes. He would tie her swollen toes together with string, hoping they might squeeze into her orthopedic shoes.

Was I destined to end up like my aunt? Fear gripped my heart.

Work became increasingly difficult. After staying home to raise my son for many years, I had just begun a career as a conference planner. Though demanding, I loved my job. The frequent travel, tight deadlines and long days, however, were taking their toll on my body. My knees swelled until they were barely recognizable, making it difficult to walk even a few yards. My fingers, puffy and red, looked like fat sausages. When I would shake hands with others, I found myself wincing in pain. Even lifting a glass of water at dinner was a challenge. Because my hands were so swollen, I was often clumsy, spilling water all over the table or myself.

It soon became clear that I could no longer carry out the responsibilities of my position. Emotionally, I struggled to come to terms with the reality.

Where is God in all of this? I wondered. I felt angry and abandoned.

For many years, I had battled physical problems. Back problems, depression, and intestinal abnormalities sent me to the hospital for days at a time. The last few years had been good—until my diagnosis.

In prayer, I railed against God. "Haven't I had enough pain in my life, Lord? What do you want from me? I've given you my entire life!"

There was no word from heaven, and no peace in my heart. Instead, the losses continued to mount.

One of the greatest pleasures in my life was my involvement with the teens at my church. Meetings, retreats, and inviting girls to my home provided many wonderful opportunities to share God's love. One evening while talking with a teen, I realized in mid-conversation that I had no idea what she was talking about. Distracted by the pain, I had not heard most of what she said!

Lying in bed that night, I let the tears flow freely while I prayed.

"God, I don't understand. I'm making a difference in their lives. Working with teens brings me such joy. Please don't take this from me, too."

Silence.

Confused and discouraged, I gave up my role as a youth leader.

I never anticipated I would be asked to relinquish my friends too. One afternoon, I was planning to go to a Van Gogh exhibit with a friend that I had not seen for awhile. As instructed by my doctor, I told her that my symptoms might make it necessary for me to rest periodically throughout the day. Her response stunned me.

"I'm afraid that will really slow us down. Maybe you should go on your own another time."

Her words caused me more pain than the disease ever could.

I soon found myself canceling plans with other friends, often at the last minute. The unpredictable nature of the disease made it impossible for me to know how I would feel day to day or even hour to hour. Eventually, they stopped calling.

My world was slowly shrinking.

Medications

The medications prescribed presented their own unique challenge. I gave myself a weekly injection of methotrexate, a drug commonly used in chemotherapy. Though the dosage is much less when given for rheumatoid arthritis, my hair began to fall out in handfuls. Within hours after an injection, I was struck by debilitating fatigue, spending the next few days in bed.

My husband was wonderful, doing all of the grocery shopping, wash and much of the cleaning. However, I could see he missed the wife he once knew.

My son had a difficult time. One afternoon after I gave myself an injection, I was lying in bed when my sixteen year old son gently knocked on the door. He poked his head into the room, paused, and quietly said, "I don't feel like I have a mom anymore." I could see the tears in his eyes. Embarrassed, he closed the door, and I could hear his feet padding down the hall to his room.

I was heartbroken.

God's Goodness

While feeling particularly low one morning, I reached for my Bible. In need of comfort, I began to read. I came across a familiar verse. "For I know the plans I have for you, declares the Lord, plans to prosper you and not to harm you, plans to give you a hope and a future" (Jeremiah 29:11). Then it hit me! God still has plans for me—even with a chronic illness.

Encouraged, I began to pray and ask God to reveal His plans for this season in my life. I asked God for "... hidden treasures, riches stored in secret places..." (Isaiah 45:3a).

God's peace slowly filled my aching heart.

Beauty for Ashes

Over the next few days, I came to realize that though I might be limited by chronic illness, God is not. He is able to bring beauty out of the ashes of chronic illness. New doors for friendship and ministry opened.

As a mentor for a Christian ministry, I respond to requests for prayer and biblical counsel online. While sitting at my computer, I have traveled all over the world, sharing God's hope and comfort.

Now that I no longer work full time, I have also joined a women's Bible study. Deep bonds of friendship have been forged as we study God's Word together and share our lives week after week.

My husband and I have recognized the importance of spending time together away from the daily routine of the illness. Although not always the case, our marriage was made stronger by chronic illness and the challenges it brought our way.

My son continues to struggle. I pray for him and trust God to complete what He has begun in my son's life. Although it grieves me to watch some of my son's choices, I know God will use this difficult time in his life for good.

God also had a special surprise in store for me. As a young woman, I dreamed of writing for publication. But marriage, raising my son, and the daily responsibilities of life made it difficult to pursue. At the time, I was content to lay it down to care for my family.

After my diagnosis, I felt a nudge from the Holy Spirit to study writing. I signed up for an online course and shortly after, made my first submission. It was accepted! It was the first of a number of articles and stories accepted for publication and the launch of my writing and speaking ministry. Through my writing and speaking ministry, I have had the privilege of ministering to hurting people in thirty-two nations.

God surely uses the weak to confound the wise, so that the glory is His alone.

Jars of Clay

Chronic illness and pain had made me feel that my life had little value or beauty. Yet, as I read the Bible, I was reminded that God delights in placing His precious treasures in clay jars and sees the treasure inside!

"But we have this treasure in jars of clay to show that this all-surpassing power is from God and not from us" (2 Corinthians 4:7).

In biblical times, it was customary to conceal treasure in clay jars, which had little value or beauty to attract attention. Though I may feel like my illness leaves me with little value or beauty, God looks at me and sees the treasure inside!

Living with chronic illness is not easy. It brings with it many losses and changes, but it has also brought with it opportunities for new beginnings. Though much has changed in my life, God has not. He still has good things planned for me—even with chronic illness.

Surrounded

Ken

I have never been so sick in my life! It started with what seemed to be a common stomach virus. Within 24 hours, I was admitted to the hospital. This began a journey that I have never walked before. I've been sick. Don't get me wrong. However, nothing of this magnitude had ever entered into my world. The doctors told me that my intestines were twisted and this had caused a blockage.

I had two choices. The first was to have my stomach pumped for a week to relax my intestines and hopefully relieve the blockage. The other option was major surgery. I opted out of surgery with the hope that the pumping procedure would fix the problem. Unfortunately, surgery finally became my only choice.

Altogether, I spent twenty five days in two different hospitals. Thankfully, the surgeon was able to find the problem and correct it, but all of this came at a price. Recovery took much longer than I expected. I had lost forty pounds and was extremely weak. I hadn't eaten solid food for over a month. At first, even the sight of a small bowl of applesauce was overwhelming to me. Because of the degree of my pain, I couldn't do anything by myself. Unfortunately, my sickness came right at the heart of my boys' baseball season. I missed most of their games, and I wound up missing seven weeks of work with no paid time off!

This experience took a great toll on me and affected me on so many different levels. As I recently sat and reflected on it all, I asked myself the question that so many who face hard times ask. How did I make it through all of that? Immediately, a word popped into my mind: people!

I had people surrounding me and supporting me in so many ways the entire time. I would have never come through it all like I did without them. Who were all these people and where did they come from? The first line of support was my family. My wife was by my side throughout this ordeal. She made sure I was never alone at the hospital, and she advocated for me when speaking with the doctors. My extended family was also a huge support. My in-laws came and watched our children several times for extended periods of time, and my parents also spent a lot of time taking care of our kids.

I also received support from my friends. Soon after the word got out that I was sick, we began receiving cards with encouraging words and financial support. Amazingly, through everything that happened, we never lacked anything. In fact, the amount of money we received covered all seven weeks of the salary I lost plus another two months of health insurance.

While I will probably never understand why all of this happened to me, there are some things I learned from the people that surrounded me. Hopefully, these truths will be an encouragement to you or someone you love who is facing a similar difficulty.

First and foremost, I was reminded that God is good. So many times, life is hard and is filled with unexplainable circumstances. It's so important to distinguish between life and God. God is not the author of sickness and evil. Instead, He uses both in our lives to reveal His goodness and love to us. The people surrounding me were God's hands extended to me.

I also learned that no one should ever go through sickness alone. My wife, Cheryl, and I made a concerted effort to communicate with our family and circle of friends during that time. I believe that this is one of the reasons why they were able to support us as well as they did. Our emails and texts kept people up to date with our needs.

Finally, I learned that God always provides for His children. Again, it's important to note that our needs were not met in some mystical way. God used our family and friends to keep us afloat during a very vulnerable time. They put their faith into action by cooking meals, watching children, reading scripture, offering advice, praying, sending cards and checks, mowing our lawn, cleaning our house, and more.

It's been almost three months since my surgery, and I'm happy to say that I'm doing much better now. From a physical standpoint, I am almost 100 percent, but even more importantly, I've seen God at work in my life again. I'm sure this won't be the last time.

A Blessing From Cancer

Cathy Kiser

My story is a lengthy and complicated one. My husband and I separated twenty-three years ago this April after a twenty year marriage. We were divorced about three years after we separated. It has been a very challenging and often difficult road. I finished raising our two sons, which were twelve and fifteen at the time, but I was disillusioned with myself and with life. I made many mistakes and was not serving the Lord as I should have been. For those reasons, my boys did not receive the support and guidance they really needed from me. I was too involved with my own pain to notice theirs.

I attended some counseling sessions over the years, but real peace and freedom from my baggage did not come until the last ten years. Slowly, the Lord brought just the right job, people, and circumstances into my life to help me heal.

One of the circumstances that helped me find renewed faith and emotional healing was being diagnosed with cancer. That may sound strange, but God knows just how to reach us. In 2005 I was diagnosed with stage two uterine cancer and stage three breast cancer at the same time. I was devastated, but God used that to increase my faith in Him and make me stronger than ever. He surrounded me with wonderful Christians that prayed for me and with me. I witnessed miracles during that time that I will never forget.

Then, in 2010, I was diagnosed with stage three breast cancer again. The Lord was so close and comforting to me once again.

Even the ultrasound technician at the medical center I visited was a Christian and shared words of comfort and encouragement, as well as scripture. Only the Lord could have arranged that! This time my treatment consisted of a bilateral mastectomy, chemotherapy, and radiation for six weeks.

During that same time, my youngest son was incarcerated for a year with drug charges. I went to visit him as often as possible and prayed for miracles in his life.

I have recovered from that year of treatments, and my son has been released from jail and is working a full time job and doing pretty well. I am so thankful for every answered prayer during this past year, and I know there are more miracles to come. I am trusting the Lord in all things.

I have been looking for ways that God could use my life to encourage and help others. I asked Liz Danielsen about working in some capacity with SCSM. She suggested I first take the Divorce Group. I had no idea what to expect or how the class might help me after so many years, but I began attending a weekly session in Warrenton.

My facilitators were very friendly and easy to talk to. Each week we watched a video and discussed the topic for that night. I was amazed at how much I had kept safely buried inside me. I began to ask questions and advice and then started to utilize it in my daily life. Even after twenty-two years, God has been healing old hurts. In addition, He is giving me wisdom for handling issues that just won't go away. I know one thing for sure. Time does not heal a broken heart. Only the Great Physician can do that, and I am so thankful that He sends godly counselors to help.

I am looking forward to reaching out to others that may need support with illness or divorce. Philippians 1:4-6 is my Bible passage for 2012. It says, "In all my prayers for all of you, I always pray with joy because of your partnership in the gospel from the first day until now, being confident of this, that he who began a good work in you will carry it on to completion until the day of Christ Jesus."

The Joy of the Lord Is Our Strength

Ruth Storms

I have always enjoyed a happy, healthy life. I am married to a wonderful godly man and have four children. We are now blessed with twelve grandchildren—eleven of them are boys! Our lives have been very interesting, traveling around the world and in the United States, and meeting people from all walks of life.

Four years ago, we were at our summer home on a beautiful lake in New Hampshire anxiously awaiting the arrival of a group of young men from Teen Challenge, an organization that reaches young people who have been involved in drugs, etc. An opportunity was coming our way to entertain these young men, and I was excited to cook for them, give them some love as a grandmother and show them firsthand how God could work something beautiful in their lives.

As the week progressed, I noticed pain in my right arm but dismissed it as I truly loved giving of myself in this capacity to these boys. On Saturday, I lost the use of my arm. I could not lift it to comb my hair or pick up anything with my hand. Yes, this was quite alarming to me. I went to a chiropractor and then an orthopedic specialist. It wasn't until November of 2004, after many tests, that I was diagnosed with non-Hodgkin lymphoma. What a blow this was to a lady who had never experienced bad news of this sort.

How could this be happening to us? We felt that we'd always tried to live right, do the right things and be of help to our fellow man. It wasn't until early the next morning that reality set in and I awoke crying big sobs. My husband took me in his arms and comforted me saying, "God knows your need and with His help we will come through this challenge together."

The first course of treatment was chemotherapy. I lost all my hair, lost weight, and lost the ability to walk on my own. But through it all, I learned to trust in God's love and strength.

God never promised that our days would always be smooth, but He has promised that when we go through a valley or near death experience, He will be there for us (Psalm 23: 4). So many people are joyful when everything is going smoothly, the money is coming in, and they have nice things. But how is our attitude when we've just lost our job, don't have enough money to pay our bills or just had a shocking diagnosis? In the Bible, Nehemiah 8:10 tells us to conduct ourselves by following His word, and the joy of the Lord will be our strength.

Has every day been easy for me? Not really, but as I seek God's face, my heart is made glad. He supplies my every need. Notice I said *need*, not wants. This is something I have discovered through all of this.

When I focus on my neighbors or even a stranger and reach out to help, my situation seems so small. I receive rich blessings by attending to another's need, and God pours joy into my life. As I write this testimony, my husband and I are working in a new church in Virginia for a volunteer program that we do for His Kingdom. We help build lighthouses (churches) across our nation so others can be introduced to my Friend and Healer, Jesus.

Experience His full and abundant love by giving yourself over to the caring of your Heavenly Father. He wants to meet your every need.

Grieving and the Chronically Ill

Diane Fritz

Most people think of grief as resulting from the death of someone—a spouse, parent, child, a friend, or even a pet. We also grieve over the loss of a job, a promised retirement, health insurance, our house, our church (friends and pastor), or family relationships. A lot of things go wrong. In chapter one of Job, he appears to lose everything. It was a time for grieving. He lost his livelihood (flocks) and his children. People believe that grief goes away, and all the pain will soon be forgotten.

However, we see in chapter two that Job lost his health, too! His three friends came to console him, but in doing so, they told Job that his calamities were because of sin. They informed him that if he would confess his sin, God would heal him.

Most chronically ill people can identify with Job. Well-meaning friends frequently tell us that if only we would confess our sin, God would heal us.

"My grace is sufficient" in 2 Corinthians 12:9 is a very hard passage. I almost wish there were sins I could confess and then be healed physically. Healing would mean I could do those things I can no longer do. Instead, I must accept that His grace is sufficient and deal with my untimely disability, loss of my job, and the ability to work. I can no longer volunteer for future projects because I don't know what my health will be. I'm also unable to play with or carry my children, or be the spouse I feel I should be. Even family and church gatherings are exhausting, and I am no longer the life of the party.

Paul did not let things stop him. He continued to glorify Jesus. I am not Paul, but I can still glorify Jesus and write about His love and grace.

CHAPTER 3

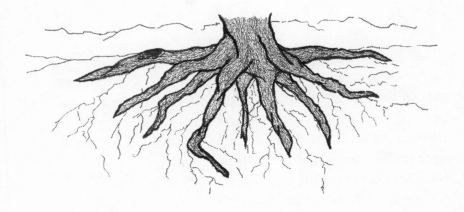

Relying on the Roots

We have come full circle and are back to the reliance on the roots to provide our needs in order to thrive and flourish. God waits patiently for us to turn to Him and call His name. It is amazing to hear these stories of pain and realize that they all go full circle back to God.

The following stories portray a reliance on God that takes the reader through situations and losses that were released to God and healing occurred. God is our Redeemer.

How a Rotten Cheeseburger Changed My Life

Tom Redmond

Just a little over a year ago, I was beginning to enjoy some of our summer church activities, especially our annual water baptism picnic. I will never forget that sunny day last June. Church members packed a friend's house and gathered by the pool for the usual summer grazing of hamburgers, hot dogs, and everything else I should have stopped eating at the age of forty.

After "dipping" ten new souls into God's wonderful kingdom, I thought it quite appropriate to dip into another cheeseburger. That was a mistake. Within minutes, I began to get a stomach ache that felt like someone lit a blow torch in my small intestine. It was quite embarrassing to ask one of my friends to take me home before my own water baptism party had ended. However, I knew something was wrong because this wasn't your normal gastrointestinal disagreement.

Over-the-counter medications did nothing to relieve the pain, and like most tough guys, I tried to wait it out. About a week later, the *tough guy* landed in the emergency room at 3am. Now, at this point in the story, please remember two things. One, make sure you are very specific with the doctor about your symptoms. Anything less leads to the second thing. "Mr. Redmond, we're going to run some tests." No, no, no! I could not stand to hear the proverbial "cha-ching" of the hospital cash register as they began to poke me with needles and offer me drinks that glowed in the dark.

Thank goodness I took the tests. They revealed a nasty blood-borne bacteria that could do serious internal damage unless I began a regimen of antibiotics that could kill a horse. And if that was not enough, the doctors informed me I would need more tests and lots of them. In fact, my health was at a point that I asked my church leadership team for a favor. I asked them for a sabbatical.

The team was gracious, giving me six weeks off, but with one stipulation. They asked me to seek out and attend spiritual counseling. The minute I heard that, I got a bit defensive. "I'm sick in the stomach, not sick in the head," I thought to myself, but I had it coming. The truth was that my wife had been after me for some time to get some counseling help with our church ministry, and now I had a perfect opportunity, but where would I go?

Thank goodness for helpful friends. In the midst of my sickness, a prayer partner sent me information regarding spiritual counseling. You see, my sickness was, in many ways, just a starting point. Spiritual counseling gave me a safe haven to both discuss my sickness and serve as a sounding board for my concerns as a pastor. Let me be honest here. *I was not going to counseling on my own. I did not need it.* I was wrong on so many levels. Just a few weeks with Liz revealed deeper issues than a stomach ache, including the need for healing from past relationships.

God is good, isn't He? There is truly wisdom in godly counsel. I needed that help before I became too discouraged. I'm doing better now. So, let me encourage you to get some help, too. You deserve it. If you are burned out, don't throw in the towel. First, make a call to get spiritual counseling. You won't regret it. Oh, and stay away from the cheeseburgers.

For Love of a Dog

Patricia Slaga

My husband, Paul, went to his office on a Saturday morning in late March 1999. Coming home, he called to say there was a large yard sale and he would stop and browse. I quipped back, "Bring *me* something!" When he sauntered into the house carrying a box of odds and ends, I teased, "Where's *my* special find?" "Look in the truck," He said. Checking out the truck and finding nothing, I ran inside. "There's nothing in your truck. Are you teasing me?" "Smiling, he said, "Try the cab." Trooping to the truck again, peering inside, I saw two small eyes looking up from the floor. "Aw, honey, you're something special!" I said. That began a twelve and a half year relationship with our German Shepherd named Hunny. It seems that a pet owner whose female AKC registered German Shepherd jumped the fence had a "romantic encounter." The owner was giving the pup away. The next stop was the dog pound. It seemed the mother had gone into the woods to have puppies but came out with one.

Hunny became our "child." She went where we went and seemed always to be under foot. We built a cabin named Sanctuary in the Virginia mountains in 2005. Every weekend we were supervising construction or rolling up our sleeves and putting sweat equity into our dream. Oftentimes in winter with glassless windows in a roughed-in structure, we bundled on a floor mat under piled-high blankets where the three of us slept! Talking, as icy smoke puffs blew in the sub-freezing air, we often remarked, "Are you sure this is just a 'one dog' night?"

There was never a time when we ventured up to Sanctuary when our Hunny was not sitting between us. She learned the exits and when at our turn-off, she would stand, barking, as if to say, "We're almost home." We never said the word "river" in ear shot of Hunny as she'd run to the door, ready for river sport! Sometimes we would leave Sanctuary early Sunday and attend church. Hunny became well socialized as folks would come to the truck after services to pet her.

Our first grandchild was one year old when we adopted Hunny. When in our care, Hunny was always just a few feet away. As the number of grandchildren grew, Hunny took on the role of nanny and slept at the foot of their bed when they were sleeping over, taking her watch until they awoke. If one of the children slept in our room, Hunny would make her rounds, putting paws on the crib and peering into their faces to make sure they were tucked in tight. The myriad hugs and romps throughout the day was her greatest joy! In later years as they grew, she became the most treated dog. Clearly she could become a poster child for Milk-Bone! She continued as vigilante, especially at the cabin, and would alert us with different growls or barks when deer, raccoon, or two-legged animals were in sight or smelling distance. She was our protector, too!

Four months shy of her thirteenth birthday, Hunny began having problems ambulating. X-rays revealed her vertebrae deteriorating and hindering use of her hind legs. With medication, she rallied a short while. As she fell often in a wobbly gait, we'd pick her up and assist her in maneuvering steps. There was no evidence of pain. However, that quickly changed, and she began having attacks of tremors and panting, indicating severe pain. Little could be done. Pain medication allowed sleeping, yet only to awake to constant hurt. A multitude of prayers were spoken on her behalf. We believe strongly God cares for all of His creation. When caring for previous pets, He responded with grace, protecting them when they feared thunderstorms. He directed us to their location when they strayed, and His healing touch was upon them in affliction. Hunny, too, was intensely afraid of rain and thunderstorms. The last night she was with us, there was a freak storm and as she lay close by us on the carpet, no longer able to jump into bed, we awoke to sounds of fear. Paul put her on our bed until the storm passed. She was still able to squirm and wiggle her fifty-seven pound frame to lie between the two of us, where, not unlike a young child in their parents' bed, she drifted off in sweet slumber.

We sought His mercy for Hunny. He gave us assurance there was only one option—the ultimate act of love for her. That decision would put us in need of His peace, as it would break our hearts. I prayed, "Oh Lord, let this cup pass from us, taking it out of our hands." That was not to be. On November 17, 2011, we "put down" our beloved Hunny, choosing cremation. Reading scriptures, praising God for the many gifts Hunny had given and multiple joys loving her had brought us, and then reaffirming we would see her in heaven, we buried our best friend at our beloved Sanctuary—her happy place.

Lessons Learned From Job Loss

Ken

On Monday, November 9, 2009, I had an experience I hardly expected and never will forget. It was a typical Monday afternoon. My assistant and I were chipping away at the myriad of things that needed to be done for the week. As a worship pastor, there is never a lack of things to do!

I was just about to pack up my belongings to leave when my office phone rang. It was my boss, the lead pastor. He invited me to come to his office to chat before I left. I soon found out that our "chat" was much more than a time for small talk. He informed me that the church was downsizing their staff, and he would no longer need my services.

That day, I started down a road that I've never traveled before. As a pastor, I've helped people who were unemployed and did my best to understand their pain. I can now say that I know their struggles firsthand. Here are some of the lessons I am learning in this new chapter of my life. Hopefully, they will be a source of wisdom and encouragement to you.

The first lesson is to learn to manage your emotions. Like any loss, my journey started with many negative emotions. I first felt denial which soon led to blame and anger. I reasoned, "How could such an injustice happen to me? I was a faithful employee, always doing more than I was asked to do. How could an organization, a church nonetheless, devalue me this much? How could God let this happen?"

My anger then led to sadness and self-pity. I saw myself as the victim in the story. I couldn't stop dwelling on what had happened.

I replayed the incident endlessly in my mind, trying to pinpoint something that I could have done differently to prevent my loss. Unfortunately, like an endless cycle, my self-pity led back to blame and then to anger again.

This went on for some time before I realized what was happening and began to address my problem head on. I came to realize that feeling these emotions wasn't wrong, but letting them control me was. With the help of some dear people in my life, I began to forgive those who had hurt me. It was then that I felt the grip that my emotions had on me begin to loosen.

Another lesson is that you are not what you do. Listen to a group of men talk and one of the first questions they ask each other is, "What do you do for a living?" As men, we naturally find our identity in our careers. I certainly have found this to be true. Being without a job has made it difficult at times to find something to talk about with the guys. It also has made me feel less important around them.

All of this has forced me to take a step back and assess who I am. First and foremost, I am a child of God. I am a husband and a father. While I currently may not hold the position, I am still a pastor and a worship leader. These are all gifts from God, and they leave me with much for which to be thankful. Lately, I find myself talking to my friends about some of these treasures in my life. It's a good reminder that I am not what I do.

Another lesson I have learned is that God keeps His Word. Job loss often leads to extended times of waiting. In some cases, job seekers search for a year or more. As one who is currently living in this reality, I have found the waiting process to be frustrating and even draining at times. The hardest part has been dealing with employers who promise to call back and never do. We live in a day and age where many people no longer keep their word. This kind of treatment can make a person feel like no one really cares at all.

Lately, I've been dwelling on the fact that God always keeps His Word. Read through the scriptures, and you will find that God has a great plan for His children and that He always follows through. God operates in a way that is in stark contrast to those looking for someone to hire. He will come through in His perfect time. And in the meantime, He will give you strength to wait if you ask Him for it.

The final lesson I have been learning is to worry less and pray more! Being without a job can definitely put a strain on the finances. As men, we are usually the main providers for our families. Not being able to fulfill this duty naturally causes us to worry about our future. Believe me—I've spent a good number of hours lying awake at night worrying about my family!

One thing that has helped me to break this habit is to remember that worry does not change my situation. If I am doing all that I can to find a job and trusting God with my situation, I need not worry. When I begin to worry, I do my best to turn it around by praying and asking God for help. As for my finances, God has been and still is providing for my family in some pretty unusual ways. I wish I had time to tell you all of it!

Perhaps you have recently lost your job like me. Whatever you do, don't give up! Remember that there are many others fighting the same battle as you. Better yet, you can be sure that God is with you and is helping you find your next job. Even when it seems like He is not there, He is working out a good plan for you. His silence is not His absence. Reach out to Him, and you will find all you need.

Unexpected Blessing

Steve

Several years ago, I heard commercials for a Grief Group on our local Christian radio station and knew right away that it was a ministry I wanted to be able to provide to our community. Little did I realize that there were some areas in my life that I hadn't completely walked through relating to grief, and I soon found myself in an unexpected position of student. In addition to personal growth in my own areas of loss, I quickly recognized how differently each person grieves and it's helped me to be far more empathetic towards others who may deal with grief differently than I.

I have suffered much loss over the course of the last ten years. I lost the only grandparent I ever knew. Shortly after that, unbeknownst to me, my wife no longer was interested in marriage and chose to leave the relationship. Then in 2009, I lost my brother-in-law to cancer, followed quickly by the birth of my son and the unexpected death of my father from a massive heart attack.

Each of these life events brought on a large variance of emotion and struggle as I tried to figure out how my life would change with each one. Although I never sought professional counseling, I was surrounded with an amazing group of friends who loved, prayed, and counseled me when I needed them. I attribute so much of my recovery to their faithfulness to support me with a godly kind of love.

I would say the initial hardest blow I received was the decision of my wife to walk away from our marriage. Not only had she been my best friend, but also my ministry partner. Like everyone else, I thought I would be married to her for life. When I got the news, I felt about as lost and confused as anyone I've ever known. Despite all my attempts to woo her back, she had already made up her mind to start her life over, which meant a new chapter would begin in my life. To the glory of God, I have been blessed abundantly more than I could ask or imagine as God not only gifted me with the greatest wife, friend, and helpmate, but in these midlife years that I'm living in, He also gave me a miracle son. If I can encourage anyone through grief, please know that although I didn't walk through everything perfectly, I did my best to honor my covenant before the Lord. Through the process, I can say that He has more than restored to me everything that had been lost, as He does for each of us that put our hope in Him.

My next season of loss came seven years later, in 2009, when my forty-nine year old brother-in-law was diagnosed with cancer that rapidly spread throughout his body. Not only was it hard watching him go through the process of dying, but it was difficult knowing that he was going to leave behind two preteen boys and a wonderful marriage to my sister. His cancer came about as a result of smoking. I have been angry for a long time at how that one addiction led to the loss of a great husband, father, and friend, and it all could have been prevented by one important decision. My sister and her two boys are doing well, but each time we meet there is still the emptiness of his presence.

My son was born the same month that my brother-in-law passed away. In a season that ordinarily would have been exciting for the family, it was the daily reminder that a great family member was gone. Then, in October, my dad suffered a massive heart attack doing what he loved to do most, bowling. What I've found in my own experiences to date is that whether someone close to you dies unexpectedly or not, the grieving process is difficult because someone you care about is gone. My dad was the guy that I would go to for counseling on certain matters, and I was looking forward to him being a grandfather to my son. Not having that person anymore has certainly left a hole in our lives.

After ten weeks of going through SCSM Grief Group, I found that there were areas that God needed to do some chiseling in my own life. I needed to hear from the experiences and testimonies of others in the video series and in the class. I am grateful for the work and ministry of SCSM and all the staff and volunteers that make it possible for this ministry to be in the community.

Burden or Calling?

Virginia Wright Rapin

I am no different than you. We were all born to our parents and expected to live a good life. However, we may differ in the various paths our lives have taken.

Being born into a family of loving parents in rural Fauquier County, I learned hard work ethics and to do without many of the finer things in life. Most importantly, I learned respect for elders, those ill and suffering from unwanted problems in their lives as they aged. Being raised in a Christian home, I learned the true meaning of loving, respecting, and honoring your parents.

As I think about family history, I am so happy that I have fond memories of all four of my grandparents. They were not just people who I would see every once in a while when they visited or on special occasions. They were a part of my everyday life as they lived very close to us, and we visited them often. For my grandfathers, I, as a very young girl, remember them more as older men who were frail and needed a lot of care by their wives and my parents. Seeing them and loving them gave me a great appreciation for our family bond through an unending love. I was older when my grandmothers suffered from age and illness, and I better understood the caregiving my parents would give to their parents.

Love comes in many forms. We are attracted to it in people in many ways. I found love in my husband who was older than me and very loving. Almost overnight, after ten years of marriage, I found myself being the caregiver to my husband who had been very healthy all his life. Over time he had greater needs as Parkinson's disease took a stronger hold on his body and he became like the child we did not have. Love calls you to be what you need to be.

I did not have training for this as I had worked in the business field. I did not have time for this as I was working a full time job and now assumed his job tending the farm as much as I could because he was no longer able. But you take each day for what it is and make the best of it. Over time he could not drive to attend his appointments alone, so it was necessary to become more involved. With the frail body, it became necessary for him to use a wheelchair, and he was not strong enough to master the wheelchair for himself. Later, as his health condition worsened, it was necessary to do more personal things for him. In my case, even among the burden of hard work, I felt I had a calling.

In the course of the day you do what you have to do and make the best of the hours you have. By the end of the day, there would be many things left undone, but you are so exhausted from trying that you fall asleep not even thinking about them. Because of love for another, you do what you had to without even thinking about it.

Many times I felt so alone. No one seemed to understand. I did not know where to turn for the help I needed. I was not alone though as I had my biological family and had a spiritual family of some dear Christians who came to our house for a Bible study. I needed resources but did not really know what might be available nor did I have the time to check it out. When I tried, it seemed to end nowhere. No returned phone calls. Not as many resources were available in the early 1990s as we have today.

With the aging population growing, there are many more resources available today. I now have both of my parents living with me. Both are facing aging issues, and I see each day that I must play a bigger role in their care. This has guided me to lead, through Spiritual Care Support Ministries, a caregiving support group for those who may be facing the same challenges that I have, am, and will be facing.

CHAPTER 4

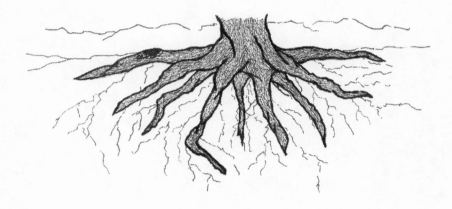

Discovering the Roots of Strength

The roots of a tree provide it with the sustenance and nourishment required for life, just as God sustains and nourishes the soul, mind, and body of each person who relies on Him. The following stories portray our reluctant nature and our resistance to the calling of God. Although we realize that God is the sustainer of all life, we are sometimes hesitant to heed His call. God, however, will be heard.

The Long Walk

Anonymous

I found myself sitting in a jail cell. This isn't allegorical; it was an actual six by eight foot jail cell. I was in such emotional agony. My entire world was about to be shattered as I was told I would spend the next ten years in prison.

How had I gotten there? My college years were a haze of drinking and drug use. I began to sell drugs to support my habits, and I fell in love with the lifestyle. My life focus was on getting high. I thought I was successful because I could buy nice things and didn't have to work. I had a beautiful girlfriend who I loved very much. I had friends who I knew would stick by me. I thought life was great, and then I received a knock on my door.

The Drug Enforcement Agency had been watching me for some time. That morning I was arrested. I needed only to be sentenced because the evidence they had stacked against me was so great. So, there I sat in a jail cell alone. The government took my belongings. I thought my family might hate me, and I had no friends standing by me. I thought I had nothing, so I started to pray.

I had been raised in a Christian home. As a child, I went to church every Sunday with my parents and had a basic knowledge of the Bible. I knew Jesus Christ had died for me so that I could be forgiven of my sins. I knew that Jesus was my Lord and Savior just as He was for my parents and grandparents. I read my Bible in Sunday School, and I was convinced of its truth and its divine authorship. When I wanted to talk to Jesus, I could just shut my eyes, fold my hands, and pray.

However, there was no Sunday School prayer that night in the jail cell. My relationship with God from my youth had long since been buried beneath my self-centered lifestyle. I cried out to God in fear. Fear, because I knew that I was wrong. I had been denying God a place in my life. I had sinned by not honoring my God, my family, and myself. I cried because I was afraid that I was too far gone. I thought I would lose my family forever. I thought I couldn't possibly be given another chance. I prayed on and on, asking for forgiveness over and over.

After what felt like an eternity, a peace started to wash over me. The Lord could use me and I wanted Him to use me. I realized that I did have something left. The only thing that I will always have and that can't be taken from me is my God, my Lord and Savior Jesus Christ, and the Holy Spirit. I had been depending on myself and things that could never last. The prayer that night opened my eyes to the eternal relationship I have with God. My Lord forgave me of my sins.

It's been a long walk since then. At first, I noticed the Lord working in me on the little things like crude language and a need to apologize when I had wronged somebody. Gradually, God is starting to work in every aspect of my life. I read the Bible every day and am constantly blessed with new insights. I have learned to play an instrument and love to sing His praises. I am so blessed with the relationship I have with my parents. We share everything and are able to talk about our spirituality together. Although I'm still in prison, the Lord is blessing every aspect of my life. God has instilled in me, through my trials, the knowledge of what is truly important. I thank God for that night in the jail cell. I thank Him for all the hardships that I've been through because they brought me to Him. Now I know that despite any hardships or whatever this world might throw at me, even if I have nothing else, I have Him!

God's Masterpieces of Hope and Healing

Karin Kyung Lim

> *Expect great things from God.*
> *Attempt great things for Him.*
> Hudson Taylor

"Art Therapy with Korean orphans at Sung No Won Orphanage ..." This is an excerpt highlighted in my journal on October 7, 2006. This was considered to be one of those impossible dreams, one with little possibility of actually going anywhere—or so I thought.

On July 25th, 2008, I noted in my journal, "I am living in Korea *doing* art therapy with children at Sung No Won orphanage!"

My dream has become a reality! I realize this was only possible by God's all surpassing power and plan being lived out in me. There is no other explanation for it. I was once an orphan in Seoul Korea with my younger brother, Jamie. But by God's hand of protection and grace over us, my brother and I were adopted to the USA and nurtured by a loving Christian family. I am forever grateful for my family, for they provided my brother and me a gift beyond measure. Twenty seven years later, I embarked on a journey back to Seoul, with my son Xavier, to pursue a dream that was planted in my heart long before I could recognize it. Today I am working with the children at Sung No Won Orphanage, the same home where my brother and I were once orphans.

The Lord's favor and provision over our lives has been and continues to remain ever so faithful. God truly has surpassed all my hopes and dreams, beyond what I could have ever possibly imagined for myself. He made what was impossible, possible. Deciding to go to Korea was a risky venture, one that took every ounce of faith to pursue. However, I felt something stirring deep within my spirit that I couldn't ignore. As I trusted in fuller dependence upon the Lord, He led me to a deeper relationship and faith in Him, and prepared the way straight to Korea.

We arrived in Korea in September 2007 and several variables fell into place effortlessly. I obtained employment as an English teacher at Kwanghee Elementary School in Seoul. Xavier began attending the fourth grade there as well. He was matched with a warm, kindhearted English speaking teacher, and joined the school's soccer team. With time, he has made the adjustment rather well, and his Korean language skills have now even far surpassed mine. He actually translates for me sometimes!

Most importantly, we found a loving, Spirit-filled church family that has provided many friendships and opportunities to grow in faith. I now lead the Orphanage Ministry and am being stretched and challenged to rise to a new level of faith in Christ. In May 2008, I attended a church retreat and received great revelation about the Holy Spirit. I had an encounter with God in a very real and powerful and life changing way, like never before. The Pastor prayed a Holy Spirit impartation over me, and once again I felt a stirring deep within my spirit, a still small voice, spurring me on to a deeper commitment and relationship with Jesus Christ. I received many visions and felt the Lord's calling to serve Him in full time ministry with the children at Sung No Won Orphanage.

Sung No Won houses approximately fifty children, ranging from infant to sixth grade. The primary reason these children are living in the home is because of family instability resulting from poverty, abuse, divorce, etc. The children are left with deep, lasting emotional scars of rejection and abandonment. This causes an "orphan spirit" in them that fosters insecurity and distrust of others. Their greatest need is for a stable person in their lives to develop a trusting relationship and convey the everlasting love and hope of Jesus Christ. Despite how their parents have treated them, they have a Heavenly Father who will never leave nor forsake them.

"Freely you have received; freely give" (Matt. 10:8b). I believe God has brought me back to this orphanage at this particular time to minister His unfailing love to His children. I am being called to pour out the endless comfort and healing that I have so freely received. The year prior to arriving in Korea, I received training in art therapy. This training, I believe, was no coincidence, as it serves as a major vehicle to now minister to the children at Sung No Won. My year studying art therapy had profoundly impacted me, bringing to the surface years of buried emotions. Through art, I was able to access deep seated emotions and pre-verbal experiences associated with my own early loss and abandonment. This paved an avenue to receive God's healing in a powerful way, instilling a greater freedom and confidence to pursue the path to Korea. Similarly, I desire to share this experience with others, releasing them to freely express their emotions and experience a deep healing in order for greater dreams and destinies to be revealed.

When I shared with the children that I once lived at Sung No Won, and showed them a picture, there was a connection formed beyond words. Art serves as an excellent way to further connect and build trusting relationships with them, especially given the language barrier. I use a variety of art therapy activities and group exercises with them to foster trust and promote self-confidence. Each child keeps an art journal with different themes each week related to personal interests and identity. I currently meet with four boys and four girls, all fifth graders, the same age as Xavier, who has joined in serving the children. What a truly rare and precious gift to serve with my child. I have witnessed Xavier's faith and character mature in countless ways. He and the boys hit it off immediately with their soccer playing interests. He has connected to the children in the most beautiful way, and they have no doubt developed a bond of brotherhood that will continue on into eternity.

I see now much more clearly all the circumstances in my life that have led me to a time such as this. Despite my past abandonment and rejection, God has restored and brought healing so that I may now share the same comfort and grace I've so freely received. God had a destiny for my life far greater than I could have ever imagined, and I stand truly amazed at the way it continues to unfold in my life!

CHAPTER 5

Tending and Encouraging Growth

Many times trees require human assistance to maintain growth and bear fruit. Humans also require attention, ministry, and encouragement to maintain life in a positive, forward-moving manner. We tend to forget that we have the love of God, and He is waiting for us to turn to Him in all situations. We often claim self-reliance which leads to dry and broken places in our lives.

We must continue to rely on the roots of our existence. God is our solution to every problem life brings our way. We frequently need to be reminded that we are not alone.

The following are stories that show how people are comforted in various ways by God and grow in their walk with Him, and then pass it on to others.

Our Awesome God!

Susan Amato

One night when our older son, John, was five years old, we were having our usual "I'm not sleepy" time. He usually had a series of questions ready to ask so he could extend the time before I would turn out the lights and go downstairs. With the innocence of little ones, he would first ask for a glass of water and then needed a trip to the bathroom (any of this sound familiar to you?). The questions came right after that. This particular night there was a full moon, and it was shining very brightly just outside his window. The question he had for me was, "How does the moon stay up in the sky?" My first thought was that I wished his dad was home, but he was out of town on a business trip. My next thought was that I wasn't really sure how to explain how the moon stayed up in the sky. I told John that God had made the moon and the stars and that He had the power to keep them where He wanted them. That seemed to satisfy his curiosity about that subject and after a couple more questions, none as complex as that one, he was ready to go to sleep.

I was reminded of that conversation with John, who is now a father of two, as my husband and I took a walk the other night. It was a rather warm night for late March, and the sky was crystal clear so we could see many stars and the full moon shining brightly. There is something about the night sky that really speaks to the power of our God. The beauty of it all is truly awe-inspiring. To think about a Creator who can hold the moon and stars and planets just where He wants them, who can control the thunder and the lightening, and who can bring the snow in winter and the warm sunshine in the spring, is overwhelming. I can hardly comprehend that a God so big and powerful can also be so personal and caring, to the point that He knows the number of hairs on the heads of each person in the world, in every generation, and that He is with us to comfort us through life's difficult times. That kind of power is too difficult to even fathom.

I think Carl Boberg, a young German minister, must have felt that way when he wrote the poem, *O Mighty God*. Most of us know this poem as the hymn, *How Great Thou Art*, and many identify it with the Billy Graham Crusades. As I reread the words of this hymn, I could feel the emotion that he must have felt as he wrote it.

Now that spring is here, we once again experience the work of our awesome God as we watch the new leaves sprouting in the trees and buds bursting forth in glorious shades of pink, red, yellow and purple, and see the crocus, daffodils and tulips opening to the sunshine. How does this all happen so timely and beautifully year after year? Surely it must be the mighty hand of our God.

Right now in our country there is a lot of uncertainty, even fear, in just about every aspect of life. However, I find peace and comfort in knowing that nothing is a surprise to our God. He is all knowing, all powerful, and is always with us. He knows the end from the beginning and nothing is too difficult for Him. After all, He holds the moon and the stars in the sky just where He wants them to be.

God Help Me, I'm Going In!

Charissa Bowers

Everyone else was already suited up and ready to submerge. The sliver of shade disappearing into black water was intimidating enough to tempt me to pass. The tunnel was submerged. We're going through that?

My swimming skills leave so much to be desired and I enjoy living. But the idea was so cool.

I donned my goggles and slipped into the cool water powerfully rising and receding. The entrance to the tunnel was wide and well lit by the light on the other side. Deep blue silhouetted nature's sculpted coral reef and eroded rock. It beckoned me. I could do this. If I had the nerve, that is.

It was time to commit. My friend was next to me contemplating her own commitment. My heart had already decided. I'm not backing out this time. I waited for the right wave, took a breath, and submerged myself into the deep.

"Don't turn around," Andrew said. "Just keep going and you'll get through for sure." God help me, I'm going in. The force of the incoming wave pushed me to the top of the rocks. I wasn't a good enough swimmer to overcome the force of the wave and found myself scaling the ceiling. Further down. I need to get further down away from the coral. My fin slipped off as I scrambled to swim deeper.

Turn around, you're not going to make it. *Don't turn around, just keep going and you'll get through for sure.* Keep going. No time to panic. The light blue and silver white of the sky approached. There's only one way to go and that's forward.

I feel like you have to live sometimes. You have to take risks. If you don't, you never live. You never get to experience the fullness of life that God has promised us. Here's the truth: Convenience is always easy, but it is never awesome. It can never be great.

It seems, of late, that I have been standing on the edge of a precipice. What am I going to do next with my life? I know what I want. I see it just like I could see the other end of the tunnel. My heart is committed. I wait though. I wait and now I ask myself, "What am I waiting for?" I have to go. I know I have to submerge into that water and take on the challenge of my life. I may not make it perfectly, but I have to keep going. I have to keep going or else I'll die.

"If you're going to fall, fall forward," a friend told me over coffee. Fall forward, don't stop, and don't turn around. If you fall, fall forward and move towards something. See the light and move.

There are things that I do in life which I don't do well. My potential for failure is intimidating to me, but I can't let it stop me. I can't listen to the voices that tell me to stay on the edge. I can see the tunnel. My heart wants it. It was made for this. Maybe I'll submerge and find that I'm scraping the top of the rocky ceiling, lose a fin, and fight to reach the surface before my breath runs out. Maybe it will happen to you, too. What do we think in those moments about our leap of faith? Fear? Was it worth it?

The other side of the cove was refreshing. I joined my friends and felt keenly in my heart that I was the conqueror. I had made it, and I had shared an experience that would last forever. There are always friends on the other side of the journey, the ones who have gone there before. They're waiting for you, anxiously some of them, to see you take the risk. Life is so good on the other side, even the struggling in the tunnel was worth every moment.

I'm going to take a leap. I don't know how much it will cost. I don't have the full weight of the risk (probably a good thing), but I do have a heart hungry for life and purpose. I might say that God is leading me. I believe that He is. He's led me to a place where I won't succeed without Him. I'll probably scrape the top and lose a fin, but I will be moving forward in faith and purpose. God help me, I'm going in.

I Went Into the Garden Today

Judy Marquette

The winter garden is so cold and desolate. Flowers that bloomed so brightly have withered away. All that was green and growing has faded to brown and shriveled. Wind rustling dried leaves is the only sound heard. I often fear the beauty will never return.

Long before it is time, the calendar shows me spring is coming. Memories flood my mind reminding me that spring is the season that my son left this earth. A life so full of promise, just ready to bloom, was taken long before his time. The cold and desolate memories are often very overwhelming.

Oh, but when spring arrives it is so sweet to go into the garden. Peeling away the layers of leaves and remnants discarded from the seasons passed reveals new life just pushing through the earth. Tiny buds form on branches where leaves once blew away. Colorful flowers burst forth and replace the brown of winter. Sweet songs of birds fill the air and the warmth of the sun is revitalizing. There is joy seeing new birth in the garden that once seemed lost.

In this garden of life, winter will not last forever. Spring faithfully reappears with a freshness that symbolizes rebirth and new life. I am reminded that spring is the season of rebirth as Easter is the remembrance of the greatest rebirth—the resurrection of Jesus Christ. As He prayed in the garden, Jesus knew the sorrow of death was before Him, but He chose to endure immense pain and suffering on the cross so we could be reborn into eternal life with Him in heaven.

Jesus gave the ultimate sacrifice to ensure that my son is now in the most beautiful and glorious garden for eternity. I will see him again in heaven, the eternal garden of paradise that will never fade or wither; where there is no more sorrow, sickness, or pain; where the music of angels fills the air; and where every day is sweeter than the day before.

Thank you, Lord, for stretching Your arms open wide and hugging my son into eternity. It is an honor to be reminded of Your love and peace, to feel the renewal of spring, to see and smell the flowers, and to listen to the birds singing in my earthly garden until the day I join You and my son in paradise.

A Prayer Shawl Ministry

Liz Shaw

A friend of mine received a prayer shawl from a ladies' group. She shared with me that when she wraps her shawl around herself, she can still feel her husband hugging her, even though he passed away months ago. She also feels the love of Christ surrounding her, especially when she is feeling low.

In April, another friend, Ruth, lost her husband, Peter, very suddenly. Since he was in Hawaii when he died, and also because he was in the military, we all knew that it would be awhile before arrangements could be made for his funeral. One of my co-workers had shown me a prayer shawl that she had made for a widow in her church. The directions to make the shawl seemed quite easy so I decided to make one for Ruth. She was very happy with the gift of the soft, white shawl, which had been made for her with a whole lot of love and prayers tucked into every stitch.

Then I made a prayer shawl for my son-in-law's mom, Deren, to comfort her as she faced her husband's cancer diagnosis and treatment.

A prayer shawl is a rectangular garment, usually with fringes, given to those who seek comfort, or is used in formal prayer. Either way, they are inspirational and offer the hope for God's mercy to those who make them and those who wear them. A prayer shawl is prayerfully made and given to comfort someone who has lost a loved one, has a chronic illness, or anyone who is grieving for any number of reasons. I really believe that a prayer shawl warms the heart of the person who receives it and helps them to realize there are others who do care even though we may not know one another.

I began to realize there is a great need for the prayer shawls in our community. We are living in a very bad economy right now. People are healing from many different challenges and losses. They need to realize they are not alone in these struggles. Just a smile, a hug, and a prayer is all many people need, but a prayer shawl will remind them that they are not forgotten and not alone. Someone *does* love them, and that someone is our Lord and Savior, Jesus Christ.

Chaplain Liz was excited when I shared these thoughts with her. I showed her some shawls I had made, and she asked me to make some for SCSM. That's when I thought it might be a great idea if others, who also liked to crochet or knit, could help me for this new prayer shawl ministry.

One reason I am making them is to keep me out of trouble! When I'm feeling down, I have a tendency to go and spend money. If I'm sitting and crocheting, I'm creating something beautiful for someone else, and that warms my heart.

I'm not sure if my friend, Ruth, has wrapped the prayer shawl around herself or not, but I hope it will remind her that she is not forgotten and not alone. I feel that God wants me to continue to crochet as many prayer shawls as I can to help comfort people. I am just one of His many helpers and messengers.

Seeing Things God's Way

Anonymous

On January 6, 2010, after two weeks of vacation, I was dreading returning to work and did not know why. I was thinking that it was a new year but back to the same old things. What's really new about returning to work? Most of you know what that feeling is like. For me, getting up at 3:30AM is not easy or fun, and facing the frigid temperature is a different story.

It was windy that morning. After taking two buses, I had to walk one and a half blocks to get to work. While walking, I asked the Lord to calm the winds as He did the sea and to allow me to have a great day, as it was the beginning of a new year and I needed a change.

All of a sudden I felt my left ankle go inward, my left knee go towards my left, and I saw myself falling towards a snow bank that was completely icy from the cold air. I immediately put my right foot forward and pulled my upper body up to prevent the fall. At that moment, I realized I sprained my ankle and put my foot down to alleviate the pain, but then I realized I could not pick the foot up again.

I called on the Lord and said, "I have to cross Route 7 (which is twelve lanes due to the new metro) and about a half of a block to get to work. Lord, I need your strength and help for I am not able to walk." All of a sudden I heard someone call my name. I was somewhat disoriented from the pain, so I thought I was hearing the Lord. They called my name again. I looked up, and it was a carpool of co-workers asking me if I needed a ride. I stated that I did, and they made room for me in the car.

When I got to work my co-workers inquired about my injury and brought me ice. My supervisor came in and I showed her my foot. She told me I should get it checked out, and she took me to Kaiser Permanente. She stayed with me until they stated it could take three to four hours to be seen, so she returned to work. They x-rayed the foot, but due to the swelling, were unable to see the damage. They fitted me in a boot that I had to wear for two to four weeks.

My supervisor picked me up, and we went back to work. While in the car, she stated that many of my co-workers were inquiring about me and my welfare, and wanted to know why she left me there alone. When I got back to the office I was astonished and amazed at the outpouring of concern, help, and love that I saw and felt from these people that I work with. They were willing to take me home to Manassas when they lived in Baltimore. At that moment I realized I was wrong about how I was feeling, and that it was a new year and a new beginning.

My hesitation of going back to work was due to my perception of how things were going to be. I was returning to the same work environment, the same old thing. However, God had a different plan. He showed me it was different, if only I began to see things through His eyes.

Upon my arrival home, I thought of all the events that took place that day and realized how awesome God really is. He placed someone there at that precise moment when I called out to Him for help. There were people to help me throughout the day with anything that I needed, and the outpouring of concern and love was incredible for me to see. God revealed to me that though at times I feel alone, I am not alone. All I need to do is cry out to Jesus, and He is always there. He will always take care of me and provide me with all that I need.

The SCSM Grief Group has shown, allowed, and helped me to grow and depend on the Lord in ways I did not know were possible. The many wonderful handouts and scriptures used in class, and the sharing of each person's loss and what they are going through, have increased my knowledge about grief, the many emotions that are involved, and how to trust and grow in Jesus. It has taught me to see things from various perspectives, how to be more compassionate, and how to listen more.

Seeing things through God's eyes is very difficult, especially when grieving, but throughout these years as a facilitator, it has matured me and allowed me to use my experiences in helping others go through the grieving process and see things through God's eyes.

In the Garden—The Tale of the Rudbeckia

Vicki Smith

> I come to the garden alone,
> While the dew is still on the roses.
> And the voice I hear falling on my ear
> The son of God discloses.
> And He walks with me and He talks with me
> And He tells me I am His own;
> And the joy we share as we tarry there,
> None other has ever known.
> (Miles, "I Come to the Garden Alone")

My grandmother and father loved this hymn. It is no wonder that I, a native of Kansas wheat fields and lover of dark, rich dirt, am a garden girl. If you visit our Warrenton SCSM Center and look around the yard, you will see some of my blooming friends. For me, gardening is free therapy, complete peace, and relaxation. It will quickly bring you to your knees. I carry a foam pad made especially for garden kneeling. Thoughts, musings, and parables come to me there. Perhaps it is because I am on my knees communing with God's botanical creation. It's not for me to understand, but I'm sure I hear from Him there.

This brings me to our topic, the Rudbeckia. For those who are not plant aficionados, the common name is Black Eyed Susan. They come in many varieties from short to tall. The ones I have at home are three feet tall, prolific, and robust. They spread and encroach on their neighbors, the lilies and Sweet William. Last summer, during

111

the hottest days of July or August, we built a planter around the mailbox by the street at the Center. This was exciting because we could put some color on Shirley Avenue in clear view of the passing traffic. What better way to brighten someone's day for an instant and attract positive attention to our Center! After driving the last nail and adding rich dirt, it was time for the best part, planting the flowers. The Rudbeckia were the prime candidate from my yard as they were standing strong, tall, and bright. I dug up a bunch and planted them carefully in the spotlight in front of SCSM. They promptly wilted. This is not unusual for a plant that has just been transplanted, so I stopped by during the midday heat to spray the leaves. By evening, the plants seemed to straighten up and revive a bit. Being a determined gardener, I hung a sheet around the mailbox to offer some sun protection. Alas, despite my best wishes and continued care, the Rudbeckia did not thrive. It was wilted, ugly, and seemed at the point of death. Reason said, "Toss it into the trash. You have lots more at home and don't need this sickly one." It did have to go. It was not a fitting plant for front and center. I went to the garden center and bought some nice French marigolds and dug up the sad Rudbeckia but did not have the heart to send the ugly clumps to the city dump. I knew that somewhere inside they still had life. So, I cleared a corner by the drive beside the line of big lilies and stuck in the Rudbeckia clump out of sight, mulched it, and watered it through the rest of the season.

There are times in our lives when we are just like the Rudbeckia. We are strong and thriving and then some life event cuts us off at our roots and takes us to another place. We are no longer safely with all the members of our loving family. We are in a foreign land, alone in the hot sun. We are stressed. We wilt. We lose some of our leaves and do not thrive. We look dead and feel dead inside. Praise the Lord that our God has a gardener's heart! He cares for each and every one of us. He nurtures and waters. If we are not ready to shine in the spotlight, He provides a place of rest, hidden away for a season while we regain strength. He does not give up on us. He knows there is life inside.

This spring I saw no sign of the Rudbeckia but had not forgotten where it was. Carefully pulling back the mulch at the corner by the lilies, I see green Rudbeckia leaves sprouting! They are alive. I am sure that this will be a better year for them, and when the time is right, they will again shine front and center.

I, like many of you, have been like last summer's Rudbeckia, wilted and fragile. SCSM is one of the protected places that God provides where we can rest and be nurtured back to full health in body and in spirit. It was a blessing to receive that care, and now it is a privilege to help extend it to others.

Music Ministry and the Ill, Dying, and Bereaved

Rev. Robert L. Reynolds

I have been singing gospel music in private homes, nursing homes, hospitals, and low income housing projects for about twenty years. Over the years I have noticed that whatever the age of the person or the type of loss, God has used my ministry in music to touch lives by the Holy Spirit with peace, encouragement, strength, hope, and healing. Even those who do not communicate very well and do not speak that often will sometimes tell me, in very plain language and with a big smile on their face, how beautiful the song was. There are others who seem to be out of touch with the world that will sing along with me when they hear a familiar hymn, and they nod their head back and forth, enjoying every minute of it.

Holy Spirit anointed music soothes, comforts, quiets, and encourages the soul. God uses music to restore the soul (Psalm 23). King Saul was relieved of an evil spirit when David would play worship music on his harp.

The following stories are examples of how the ministry of music has been effective in helping to heal the grief wound of the ill, dying, and bereaved.

Evelyn is an elderly nursing home resident with Alzheimer's disease. I have been visiting her for about one year. She never remembers my name, but she does remember that I am the man with the guitar. One day I played for her in the hallway at the nurses' station. After playing and singing some hymns for a few minutes, a few more residents came out of their rooms to listen. By the time I left, an hour later, about ten residents and family members were listening to and enjoying the gospel music. They all thanked me for coming, visiting, and singing for them.

Fritz was a homebound, chronically ill, forty-seven year old male whom I visited for about two years. We had good conversations about his family, his past ministry, education, and how he was coping with the loss of his health and having to depend on his wife and others for his care. Toward the end of the visits, I would read scripture, sing some songs, and then pray. He always seemed to enjoy the music. Once when I visited him and his wife at a rehab facility I sang *You Raise Me Up*. Fritz started crying during the song, but by the end of it, he seemed to have received comfort from it.

June was a ninety-one year old homebound patient whom I and Chaplain Elizabeth Danielsen visited weekly. I would sing some familiar hymns during each visit. Both she and her husband, John, always said they enjoyed the hymns. The music seemed to calm them, cheer them up, and give them hope.

Another place where my ministry in music has had an impact is at Family Grief Camp. During the music time, the children and adults alike sing, clap their hands, and play musical instruments, as well as do body movements, including marching around the room. They all seem to begin to relax and enjoy the experience of family camp. This helps them begin to process their grief, mourn their losses, and receive healing from their grief wound through the rest of the day's activities. I have observed children who have come to the camp timid and sad looking, smiling and laughing by the end of the music session.

As demonstrated through these stories, God has a way of using music that is anointed by the Holy Spirit to bring peace, strength, encouragement, hope, and healing to the ill, dying, and bereaved as it soothes and quiets the soul. This allows the person to mourn their loss, experience the restoration of joy to their soul, and receive healing from their grief wound and broken heart. We should all thank God for giving the wonderful gift of Holy Spirit anointed music to minister to us in our time of grief and mourning.

In God's Eyes

Susan Izzie

My child, why do you not use the gifts I have bestowed upon you? You hide behind your insecurities and your need to please other people. I give special and individual gifts to each and every one of my children. You remind me of a miser that buries his treasures out of fear. Treasures that could benefit others, but you're afraid to share.

I see the compassion in your heart and know that you have a genuine desire to do My will. You are intimidated by circumstances. I want you to follow me without consideration for anything other than to do what I ask of you. It matters not what anyone else wants when I am the one asking. Give me your concerns and your burdens, and follow where I lead you. I know you have the ability to see the pain in others since you have weathered the storms in your own life. I have had a purpose in allowing you to experience pain. Each challenge has brought you closer to Me and has given you the strength to do My will. You are now equipped to assist others when they feel the pains of life to be overwhelming. You have been there, and you know that I am the only way.

I have given you the ability to use your voice in the written word. What have you done with it? You write book after book and close them up in a cabinet so no one can see them. These books that you write for children are a gift I have given you, yet you don't share them with anyone. Each and every poem you write holds special meaning to you. The thoughts and feelings you experienced as a child are in each and every verse. Your writings are your life's experiences in their simplest forms put to paper and hidden away. Have faith in what you write. Know that rejection is not failure. Someone will look and see the heart of your inner child in your work. They will see true childhood memories, dreams, and thoughts that you have never expressed verbally but have kept in your heart for so many years. Share what you write; it is My gift to you.

I also know your sins. These I did not give you, these you have chosen for yourself. Keep looking to the example of Jesus. He was not critical of Himself or others. He did not feel resentment when people didn't treat Him as they should. Remember, not everyone experiences feelings and emotions in the same way. You can be hurt by their harsh or unkind words when those words may not have been intended for pain.

I know that creativity and art are gifts I have given you that bring you pleasure and peace. Peace that you rarely feel in other pursuits. I love to see you do something that relaxes you and calms your heart and mind. Embrace this natural remedy for your tensions and sadness. Create to give others pleasure; create to give yourself calm.

I see your mother's heart. I know your pain in having a child away from you, but I also know what is happening to change this child's life. He will lead a godly life, a life you can be proud of. A life I am proud of. I see the pride you have in the children I blessed you with. Remember, they are yours for a time but they are Mine forever. I see the love you have for your husband and the bond you have with each other even when life is painful.

I know how much your friendships mean to you. You would do almost anything for the people you love. Now, I want to see that brought to more than just your family and circle of friends. Treat everyone with love for they are all my children.

Spend more time with Me. Your mind is always in turmoil. Stop and feel the peace a closer relationship with Me brings.

I would have you lose your inability to relax and truly enjoy the calmness of My love. Breathe slower and take time to enjoy the life

I have given you. I did not put you here to please everyone; I put you here to love everyone. Help where I need you, but don't neglect yourself, for you are My child, and I love you as you are. I don't see you as ugly or insignificant, and it saddens me that you see yourself that way. Know that I have made you just as I wanted you to be. Treat yourself with love just as you would treat someone else in need of your love. Don't allow anyone to make you feel less than what you are. You are My child, and I know who you are meant to be in your earthly life. Now, listen to the words I have impressed on your heart and follow Me.